MY MESS

TROY BLACK

INSPIRE
CHRISTIAN BOOKS

InspireChristianBooks.com

TABLE OF CONTENTS

- 1 -

I Believed I Could Fly

"I know that everything God does will remain forever; there is nothing to add to it and there is nothing to take from it, for God has so worked that men should fear Him."

Ecclesiastes 3:14 (NASB)

When I was a young child, I was prone to believe anything I imagined. I never was one to think that Santa or the Tooth Fairy were real, but when it came to fantasies that I constructed, I was willing to believe in pretty much anything. A good example of this is that as a child, I believed that someday I would stumble across an alien being or toxic chemical that would give me the ability to fly. In fact, I so adamantly believed my life was going to be filled with miraculous adventure and wonder that I ignored the fact that no one in history has ever possessed such a power. It may sound a little like I was crazy, but let me remind you of the impossible things *you* believed as a child. As kids, we find it easy to put hope in imaginary notions. As we grow older, it seems that life teaches us to accept the way things are and to compromise our childish ideas about reality.

Over time, I began to realize that not only was I currently unable to fly, but that it would never be possible. I slowly started to surrender my wild dream and exchanged it for the pressing responsibilities of the physical world. It was painful to be sure, but

I kept telling myself that I would be okay without my childish desires and that the pleasures of life would be good enough to replace the amazing adventures I had dreamed up as a young child. Keep in mind, most of this mental reconstruction occurred before I turned ten years old.

Here is the point: as children, we are willing to believe things that have little or no evidence of being true. We are able to believe what we want to believe because we deeply desire our beliefs to come true and have no reason to admit that they won't. You might be thinking, *Isn't this book about God? Are you telling me it's childish to believe in God?* Well, it is childish to believe in God, but I'll get to that point later. Every incredible, amazing, extraordinary thing that I believed as a child eventually wore away as I experienced the reality of life, except one thing: I still believe in God.

The harshness of growing up has slowly stripped away all of my childish notions about what life is except one. Instead of deconstructing my belief in God, the wear and tear of life has done the exact opposite. My belief in God's existence is stronger now than it was when I was young because my experience, not just my raw belief, tells me that He exists. So where does this realization leave me? Well, if you also believe in God, you might be thinking, *Good for you. I'm glad to see that life didn't get the best of your beliefs.*

However, the night that I first realized I could not shake my belief in God, I was looking up at a starry sky, and I was scared out of my mind. I realized that I believed in an almighty, all-powerful Creator of the universe, and it didn't make me happy at all. Instead, I almost wet my pants.

For a young person seeking to get the most out of life, the only thing more upsetting to me than the possibility of God being real was the knowledge that I actually believed He was real.

Let me try to explain. If God is real, but we have no understanding of His existence, then we have nothing to worry about until we die. We can go about our lives, pushing ourselves to find meaning in one activity after another. On the other hand, if we truly believe that God is real, then we have to presently acknowledge the fact that we will one day stand before Him face-to-face. This realization ruins everything.

In this book, you're going to hear my story. You're going to read the intricate details of my life that have tried to kill my beliefs or helped to build them. You're going to find out that a young man who feels like he is king of the world can still get the wind knocked out of him by a single word from God.

The day my life finally began to change for the better was the day that I allowed the fear of the Lord to begin to influence my decisions. If the phrase "the fear of the Lord" turns you off, then keep reading. I believe the reason this phrase can cause some of us discomfort is because we do not understand how a biblical fear of God is directly connected to the love of God. As I tell my story, I'm going to illustrate the difference between a healthy and unhealthy fear of the Lord. If you don't understand the distinction between these two, I pray that you do by the end of this book, because once that healthy fear grips your heart, your very dreams begin to change. Your views on life are morphed into a godly perspective, and I can guarantee that your life will be transformed.

You may have attended church throughout your childhood—I did. You may have prayed to accept Jesus when you were young—I did. You may have abstained from the evils of the world for as long as possible—I did. If this is you or even if it isn't, I believe God desires to speak to you through this book. I believe that He is earnestly longing for you to go deeper in your relationship with Him, and my hope is to ignite or reignite that same yearning in your heart.

For the longest time, I thought I knew Someone that I really didn't. I thought that Someone had my back when He really didn't. I thought that I was righteous when I really wasn't. It wasn't until I truly met God (and was completely terrified by the encounter) that I began to experience His love, life, blessing, comfort, character, friendship, and grace. But let me take you through it all. Then we'll come out on the other side together, and I pray that God will be there waiting.

- 2 -

Bargaining With God

A man once sat up in his bed at night, thinking about whether or not God existed. Finally, he came up with an idea. He spoke out, "God, if tomorrow everything I've ever wanted out of life happens, then I'll believe You exist. If it doesn't happen, I'll just assume You don't exist and that I was just having this conversation with myself."

So the man went to sleep, and the next day he slept in several hours later than usual. He hopped out of bed, frustrated that he was extremely late for work, when the phone began to ring. It was his boss. The man assumed that he would receive a deserved lecture, but instead his boss said, "Never mind that. Just get down here. Some crazy stuff is happening."

The man rushed to work, hitting no traffic due to the time. He found a perfect parking spot right in front of the building and headed in. His boss met him with an affirming handshake. "Congratulations!" he said. "That solo project you took on last week just caused our sales to skyrocket! I'm taking this as a good opportunity to retire, and you're getting my job. It comes with a huge raise, a spacious office, a new company car, and a personal assistant."

The man was thrilled. He was finally going to be the boss. Settling into his new office, he began looking online for a new house. He decided that his new income meant it was time for a change. A listing soon drew his eye. It was the big yellow house he had always wanted that was at the end of his block. It was for sale and at a great price.

The man got off work early and went to look at the house with the realtor. It was more spacious than he remembered, and it was cheaper than he could have imagined. He signed the papers and drove home, enjoying the ride in his new company car.

When he got home, his wife also had news of her own. She sat him down and announced that she was pregnant. "We are finally going to have a baby!" she said with excitement. The man was thrilled. In fact, he was overjoyed. They spent the rest of the day celebrating all the wonderful changes that were taking place.

Yes, for the man, life finally seemed to be offering him everything he had ever wanted. That night, as he sat awake in bed, he spoke with God once more. "Okay, God," he began. "I know a lot of great stuff happened today, but I just want to be sure. If tomorrow is just as good, then I'll believe You are real."

When I was a young boy, I used to think, *If I do this, God must do that*. Another way I went about thinking was, *If God does this, then I'll do that*. It was several years before I realized that God was going to complete what He planned on accomplishing, and I could get in on it if I wanted to. God's will is supreme. If we think we are going to change it by engaging in a bargaining system or by simply ignoring it, we are in for a harsh shock. Am I saying that we cannot influence God? Not necessarily. Later on, I'm going to talk about the way that God does allow us to influence Him. For now, my point is this: why do we expect a perfect God to bend His plans to our imperfect desires? If God suddenly fulfilled all your wishes, would it really change your life for the better? The man in the story received everything he had ever wanted out of life, but for some reason, he still had a hard time believing that God was the one behind it all.

I know this may not be an easy thought to consider, but I propose that God's plan is better than yours and mine. The concept that God knows best is easy to talk about in Christian circles, but how often do we really live our lives by that truth? I'm going to be brave and ask a harder question: if we believe that God is real, are we willing to actually give up everything and anything to follow Him?

There is a question I've had to ask myself multiple times: *is it going to take my whole life for me to accept that God is both all-knowing and perfectly loving?* I know this is an impossible question to answer because we can't see the future. However, it is a question that forces me to consider my priorities in life. It causes me to admit that I want to know God for who He is right now, that I don't want to wait any longer, and that I desire to shape my decisions around His truth. If you have a different answer to that question right now, that's okay. I didn't write this book to tell you what's wrong with your life. I wrote this book to tell you about what I've done wrong in my life because I also want to tell you about God's amazing response to my choices.

The truth is it may take your entire life for you to acknowledge that God really is in control. You may finally admit that His will is more important than your own, but by then, it could be too late, and I don't want you to get to that point. If you go through every day just like that man in the story, thinking that someday you are going to have enough evidence to believe God— or worse, to make a crazy decision like giving up everything for God—then how much evidence is it going to take? Here's what my own story has taught me about seeking God: I don't think a lack of evidence is our real problem. There's another issue going on that's keeping us from seeking Him, and I'll reveal what that is as I relate the story of how I came to know God.

One widely-used argument against the existence of God is that a loving God would not allow bad things to happen to good people, and I want you to keep that argument in mind. I'm going to take the next several chapters to tell you my story, and then I'm going explain why I believe that argument is not valid.

I have three sisters and two brothers. I could have had three sisters and three brothers, but when I was about eleven, as my mother neared the end of her third trimester of pregnancy with my little brother, something happened that changed all of our expectations. My mom and dad sat us kids down and asked us if it would be okay if our brother did not turn out the way we thought he was going to. I thought, "Yes, that's okay. I'm going to be happy with a little brother no matter how he is." My dad explained that the doctors were unable to find the little heartbeat that had for nine months been beating, waiting to be introduced into a world of loving and smiling faces. I did not fully understand the implications of his statement.

As I was driven to the hospital that night, I dreadfully hoped the doctors had made a mistake. I prayed, "God, if you let my brother live, I will serve you so much better than I ever have before." I kept coming up with more things that I could do if God would only bring my little brother into the world alive. In my desperation, I was saying, *If God does this, then I'll do that.* I wanted to somehow bargain for the life of my brother. I wanted to be able to save his life, and so I offered what I thought I had. I said, "You win, God. I'll serve you with everything I have—just save him."

What I did not realize at the time is that God created me with the ability to serve Him, and if He had wanted to force me to fulfill a specific purpose, He would have done that already. In the end, it wasn't up to me. It was up to God. No matter how much I bargained, I had no power to stop death.

My brother was stillborn.

That night, I held my little brother in my arms for the first and last time, and we buried him later that week in a nearby cemetery.

My thoughts about God after that event were few and far between. I would still read the Bible with my mom, and I would pray in the mornings, but I was scared to bring up the fact that God had not come through. My emotions felt dirty, and I feared being honest with God. Nonetheless, I experienced a sort of relief that I would not have to live up to the desperate promises I had made. I was off the hook. God had not accomplished His end of the bargain, so I did not have to undertake mine. My brother had died, so my life was my own. What I did not realize at the time was that God's will is supreme. He not only has a reason for everything He does, He has a good reason. Am I saying that God ended my brother's life? No, but He did have the ability to save his life and yet for some reason chose not to. In my small, self-centered brain, I could not see what God was planning. So, as I contemplated my future, I made plans of my own and decided to attempt to involve God in them. After all, I still believed He existed.

In the next stage of my life, I continued to operate in the bargaining system I had constructed. I believed that God was compelled to act on my behalf if I did the right things. Because I thought this notion was true, I was a very good kid. My mother homeschooled me, along with my brothers and sisters, until the seventh grade. When I began to attend private school, I was a slightly awkward, scared nerd of a junior-higher. People intimidated me. At home, I was fine. I could talk and laugh and enjoy the company of my family, but school was different. I had one friend, and we sort of stayed off of everyone else's radar. It wasn't that I didn't like people; I just could not get over the fear of being around people I did not know.

Partially for this reason, I began to take pride in the fact that I could make good grades. When the teachers would hand back my classes' test papers, they would often comment on my above-average performance. In response, I would act shy, but inside, something was forming. Something was changing. I began to live for the next A+ grade. I began to live to impress my teachers more than I had with the last assignment, and in doing this, I also began to crave the constant acknowledgement that I was better than the other students in my class. You may think, *Well, there isn't too much wrong with wanting to make good grades.* The problem wasn't with having a high GPA. The problem that was forming was a much deeper issue, one that would affect my core beliefs.

As I developed this habit of self-admiration, I also cultivated a spirit of pride. My faith in my own accomplishments branched out to infiltrate every area of my life, even my beliefs about God's character. I had read about the fall of man in the Bible, and I began to think that I could do a good enough job in life to make up for any sort of rift between my Creator and me. Again, I began to think, *If I do this, God must do that.* I attended a Christian school, so when the Bible teacher would give us a verse to memorize, I would memorize it thoroughly along with an additional verse. I relished in the idea of impressing my teachers.

All this time, I thought that I was also impressing God. I thought when I was friendly toward the unpopular kids in the lunchroom that God would be kinder toward me because I had earned it. I would wake up in the mornings and do all of my household chores while singing songs to God. I memorized verses in my spare time. I would even pray long prayers sometimes just to get God's attention. Now, I am not saying that my heart was never truly seeking God. There were times when I would put the selfishness aside, but often it was right there waiting to latch back on.

The cause of all of this was a dire one: I misunderstood God's character. However, an amazing discovery awaited me. God's true character is far better than the version of God I had contrived in my head. Because my version of Him was based mainly on the bargaining system I've written about, I thought that God was going to bless me in life because of how I had acted all of those years growing up. I thought, *I've served my time, Lord. Now it's time for You to hold up Your end of the deal.* The problem with this thinking was still the same. God was going to accomplish His plans, and I could get in on them if I wanted to. Unfortunately for me, getting in on His plans was not exactly what I had in mind. I wanted to be the one making the plans, and I thought that God could simply join in when He felt like it. It would take some major shaking in my life for me to change my mind.

When my older brother and I were very young, we often played make-believe with a collection of stuffed-animals we had amassed over our few short years. Among these stuffed animals were some cute-looking creatures and some not-so-cute ones. My brother and I naturally had our preferences, and my favorite was this one stuffed bear with a red bowtie that I called Black Bear. Before even getting out of bed on Saturday mornings, we would begin to imagine stories and adventures that our stuffed animals would embark on.

Our favorites out of the group would always be the good guys or "heroes" of the story. Our least favorites would always play the villains. At the end of every adventure, the heroes would always get the girl, find the buried treasure, and return safely home to a grand party for the whole animal kingdom. Of course, the villains would always miss out on the party since they ended up drifting off into the sea of lava on a lonely floating island. My brother and I acted as gods. We were in charge of our own little universe, and everything that happened to the creatures that lived there was solely based on our childish whims.

When I used to think about God's view of me, I believed it to be similar to the view I took toward Black Bear. Because I was in charge of my own little universe as a child, I always showed favoritism. Black Bear was my favorite, and I thought I was God's favorite. I was like a cute little stuffed animal with a red bowtie. God liked me the best, and my life was going to be blessed because of it. I was going to end up getting the girl, finding the buried treasure, and returning home to a party that everyone threw for me. Instead of assuming that God liked me because of my cute little face and soft fur, I made this assumption based off my actions. I thought, *I'm not such a burden on God as everyone else, so He must like me better than them.* Here is the strange part of the story. My thinking was backed up by the fact that God was blessing me. For reasons other than the ones I figured, the God of the universe was indeed blessing me. Even though I assumed it was because *my* plans were in motion, God still had better plans. I was eventually going to find out how scary it can be when your own plans collide with His.

As I moved into my teenage years, I changed schools and began to make more friends. My life changed dramatically. People whom I had often assumed disliked me were now magnetically drawn to me. I was still quiet and shy, but I gradually socialized to the point where I felt comfortable around most people. And because my situation was so contrary to what it had been, I began to consider myself somewhat popular.

You might assume that my newfound ability to make friends would decrease my grade point average, but that was never the case. It's funny how we sometimes need something from God, and as soon as we get it, we say, "Thanks God, I can handle it from here." When this is the case, God may have a different reason for letting you get what you want other than you simply wishing for it.

As I began the journey through my high school years, I was getting what I desired. Needless to say, I was getting it for a different reason than I had suspected. God had a plan that outweighed mine, and because of this, I would be going on a wild ride to eventually move out of my plan and into His.

- 3 -

Time To Grow Up

I've told you how I thought I was better than everyone else. Though I thought this way, I wouldn't admit the notion to myself. God was still blessing me, and I thought that it was because of what I was doing. I didn't realize it was because He had His own plans in mind.

Mediocrity was the one thing I avoided in high school. I fed a constant determination to be the best. I strove to be number one. I hoped to be remembered. Each day was a gift—an opportunity for personal expansion. My fear of people continued to subside, and so my love of attention naturally blossomed. I involved myself in sports, trying out for the basketball team and later running track and playing soccer. Over the course of four years, I acted in six plays. I attended banquets and lock-ins. In between everything else, I studied relentlessly. I began to live.

Or so I thought.

My anger toward God began to fade into the background as my circumstances changed. Life presented itself as lovely and pleasing, and so I saw God as being good as well. Because I knew that God had promised to be with me in His Word, I lived as if He always had my back. I believed that everything I did would work out because God was my aid. Then, just when I thought I had crossed over into the green pastures of happiness, I developed a crush.

Of course, I had no way of knowing what a crush was, so I naturally looked at it and called it love. I reasoned, *I've never been in love, and I've never felt this way before, so this must be love.* This conclusion probably sprouted from some principle of deductive reasoning I learned in geometry class. (For those non-math types, that was a joke.) At the time, it didn't matter how I made the conclusion. All that seemed to matter was that I was "in love." This feeling or notion that I had found love made me feel adequate. I felt like I had arrived at an understanding of happiness. The world was out there, vainly stabbing each other in the back over a slice of contentment and meaning while I had discovered it without even looking.

This girl was more than anything I had hoped for, and she was going to be my life. My beautiful illusion came unexpectedly crumbing down on the morning of April 7th of my tenth grade year. She broke my heart with a casual note passed back to me at the end of our world history class. For two weeks, my nights were spent listening to John Denver's greatest hits and re-reading *The Hiding Place* over and over as I bawled my eyes out in my bedroom. From then on, I gritted my teeth and held onto my drive to surpass the status quo more than ever before.

Like I said earlier, as children, we are able to believe things that have little or no evidence of truth. Because I did not want to lose this childlike belief, I had often told myself that I would never grow up. This high school breakup, though, was the point when I began to forget the heart of my beliefs. I could've simply believed that God was going to provide me a wife of noble character whom I would love and cherish for the rest of my life, but I didn't. I chose not to believe. I decided this because of my bitterness associated with losing the girl I had deemed "the one." I thought, *God, she's right here. Can't You see?* I thought I was instructing God on what He had intended. I could see the girl that stood before me. What I could not see was the woman God would lead me to marry. I had no picture of her. Because of this, I went with what I could see. I became furious toward God for letting her get away.

The weird thing about my mental picture was that I was only sixteen. Boy, was I a genius. I thought that if God couldn't handle it right then, He wouldn't handle it at all. I let myself be overcome with bitterness.

Bitterness is worse than sorrow because it eats away at you long after genuine sorrow has passed. I was unhappy, but worse than that I had opened my maturing heart to the cancers of cynicism and skepticism. A young heart is a strong heart. The older a heart is, the more blood it has pumped, the harder it has worked, and the more stress it has endured. I began to wish that there was a way my heart could be made new. I began to wish that there was a way *I* could be made new.

You should never allow yourself to fall so much in love with something or someone that it's not okay for God to take it back. I'm not saying that every bad thing that happens is God's doing, but let me remind you that He has the ability to stop bad things from happening. He is all powerful, but we also live in a sinful world full of mistakes and pain. God could reach down and stop any evil thing from happening, so why doesn't He always do that? If we live a good life, don't we deserve for good things to happen to us? This is what I believed, and it was this very belief that drove me to reject God's plan. In my mind, there was no way that God had a good reason for allowing things to turn out the way they did. I had lived a "godly" life, and yet God had let me down. Looking back, my hardships paled in comparison to the lives of some, and yet they still drove me to bitterness. I know I'm asking questions that I'm not answering yet, but I want you to think about this for a little while. Would you still love God if He allowed you to lose the best part of your life?

That's what had happened to me. I had lost the one thing in life that I wanted most. I had given my allegiance over to someone who had produced good feelings inside of me instead of to the One who had created me. I don't think it's possible to lose belief altogether. You simply choose to put your belief in something else, oftentimes in a lie. As a hurt, disregarded young man, I chose to believe what my feelings were telling me, and I oriented my belief away from what God had told me in His Word.

I gave in to the idea that I had been done an injustice. Ultimately, I gave myself over to the idea that my rejection was the result of an error on God's part. Then, I submitted to the notion that I would live the rest of my life as a reject because of one "mistake" made by one young lady. I didn't realize that Jesus meant what He said when He taught that you must hate your wife to love Him (see Luke 14:26).

I'm not saying that Jesus wants husbands to hate their wives as you might hate someone who you immensely dislike. Instead, Jesus was painting a picture. Our devotion and love for God should be so great that no other commitment or desire in our lives should even be comparable. Nothing we possess and no person we care for should be able to extinguish our faith in God. God desires for us to love and trust Him that much. Instead, I gritted my teeth at Him for allowing me to lose my desired wife. However, even though I had pinpointed the fault on God, I tried my hardest to point all the anger I felt away from Him. Because of the extent of my hatred and bitterness, I eventually chose to blame not just one young lady but the entire female sex.

You might be thinking, *That isn't fair. It would've made a whole lot more sense to blame God, since you ended up at the idea that it was His fault anyway.* Yes, that is true, but I still didn't want to get on God's bad side. I had not lost hold of the belief that God was in control of the universe. I still wanted Him to look on me with love, so I blamed women instead. I needed something to pass my anger and frustration off on in order to continue justifying myself before Someone who I had been taught was righteous. I figured I couldn't be angry with someone who is perfect. So I put everything I had against God on women. I loved God while I hated them, or so I thought.

Somehow, I felt justified as long as I didn't outwardly point the finger at God. I still worshiped God on a regular basis, but I did it with hatred in my heart. In my bitter state, I was blind to the truth: when I hated others, I was also hating God. Let me expand on that thought with a story.

Once, a man who lived in a small island village was on his way to church. The villagers would worship in the center of the island at the highest hill around. To get to this hill, the villagers would have to travel a short distance through the jungle. As a custom, they would worship God at noon every day. Just like every ordinary day, the man began his burdensome track through the thick trees. However, that specific day, he was on a mission. He had only one day left until he would lose everything he had because of debt, and he was going to ask God to save him from ruin after the scheduled worship time. As he traveled through the forest, he came upon a young lady who was attempting to carry two huge jugs of water.

"Please, sir," she begged. "Can you help me?"

The man did not want to miss the time of worship, but the woman seemed to be struggling a great deal.

"I don't have time," he said.

"Please, I'm not going far," she begged once more.

The man decided that he would help as long as her destination was nearby. He carried one of the jugs of water and began to follow her. However, as they continued mile after mile, he began to realize that they were traveling a lot further than she had made it sound.

"How far are we going?" he asked, irritated that it was taking so much of his time.

"It's not much further," said the woman.

They continued on for some time after that, but finally, the man realized that he was going to miss the traditional time of worship. He handed the woman the jug and left. Hurrying back the way he came, he finally made it to the hill where the villagers worshiped. Unfortunately, the worship time was over. The man went home, disappointed. The next morning, he lost everything he owned because of his unpaid debt. That day, he arrived at the appointed time to worship.

Throwing himself before God, he cried, "Why did You send that woman in the jungle to distract me? If I could have only arrived on time yesterday, I could have asked for what I needed. Perhaps I would not have lost everything if I had only arrived in time to ask You."

Then, much to the villager's surprise, God answered him. "It would have done no good even if you had arrived on time," He said. "Yesterday, I wasn't here. Yesterday, I was in the jungle carrying jugs of water. It's not that you didn't arrive on time. You simply left too soon."

"Truly I say to you, to the extent that you did it to one of these brothers of Mine, even the least of them, you did it to Me."

Matthew 25:40b

When we are so focused on being religious that we forget to love one another, we can end up praying and staring off into the darkness wondering why God hasn't taken the time to answer. I thought that because I was a "godly" person in most areas of my life, I was justified in treating women however I wanted. Now, I did not consciously consider this thought, but I did justify my bitterness toward them by measuring it against the good deeds that I performed for God. This was a serious problem because bitterness can cause you to do regretful things you never thought you would do. When that bitterness is fueled by self-justification, you find yourself in a dark place.

I had a dream one night where I sat in a shadowy room that was filled with friendly people. I began to speak with them, and at first I was content to converse with them. However, after a little while, the darkness began to annoy me. It was difficult to see what was around me, and I had trouble recognizing people's faces. So I asked one man whom I had been speaking with if he would join me in seeking out a room that was better lit.

The man in the dream responded, "I prefer the dark, actually." I looked at him with disbelief.

"Well, I prefer the light," I said. "I'm going to go find it."

I left and began searching. I searched desperately, climbing ladders and moving through hallways. Eventually, I arrived at a room that was well lit. There weren't as many people there. They all seemed to be working on something important, but I knew that I was in a better place because I could see.

When I think back to this dream, I see a picture of a person who was fed up with living in crippling darkness. I believe that's where some of us are in our relationship with God. We pray, attend church, and read the Bible, but God's plan for our future is never revealed. We listen to worship music that talks about God being with us, but we hardly ever experience His closeness.

It's time that we get tired of the dark. It's time that we get tired of not being able to see. It's time that we get tired of not knowing where we are going or whether or not God is actually with us. As I let the bitterness surround me at the end of my second year of high school, I thought I knew who was with me. I thought that I could see clearly, but I was really staring off into the darkness, wishing I could see just a little further. Unfortunately, it was still going to be a while until I realized just how greatly I needed the light.

During my senior year of high school, I still wrestled with the idea that God had messed up. I no longer felt as bitter because I had decided that I was going to give God a chance to fix the mess He had created. However, it had to be one swell fix, or I wasn't going to accept it. A depressing idea lingered in my mind: If God finally attempted to make things right, I toyed with rejecting His plan and throwing His blessings back in His face. Then, perhaps He would understand how He had made me feel. *Now He will see. Now He will understand the pain He caused me.*

These thoughts of getting even with God were so prevalent that I eventually decided to follow them. When the chance finally came around to date the young woman that had disregarded me two years earlier, I said no. Though I had learned to bury my feelings bitterness had taken over my heart. Instead of saying yes to the girl that I cared for, I went out and dated someone else because I thought that it would be fun. I believed the lie that one relationship can make up for another. I was too young and too oblivious to the idea of cause and effect to realize that my actions would create a bigger impact than what I had planned.

Did I like the girl I chose to date? Yes and no. She was beautiful and fun to be around, but the whole time I knew that something just wasn't right. I realized this more than I was willing to admit to myself. The real reason behind my actions was supposed freedom. If I had been trusting God, I would have waited until I knew that I was ready to date, but I wanted to be the one making the decision. In the same way that God had let me down in allowing my infant brother to be a stillborn baby, God had let me down when it came to His job of providing me the girl of my dreams. This thought revolved around my assumed rights. God had not followed the plans written out in *Troy's Rulebook of Life*, so I didn't have to follow His.

I still did not think that it was morally right to be an evil person. I simply thought that I was okay in God's eyes because I was not committing the sins that I would have classified as unforgivable. Because I had not stooped to engaging in those sins, all my other actions were justified in my mind. God had not held up His end of the deal, so I didn't have to hold up mine. I looked at my future with anticipation because I had learned how to live in freedom. Or so I thought. The truth was that I was chained down by sin, and I was too blind to see it.

Though I was not about to let *myself* get hurt by love again, my new girlfriend did not carry the same mindset about our relationship. She thought that I was as devoted as she was, or at least that I cared about her genuinely. I did not comprehend until a long time later the damage that I created in my rash actions.

I dated her for a while, and then when I didn't want to date her anymore, I told her I just didn't care. I told her I didn't care, and I left. I was looking out for my own skin, and I ended up hurting someone that should not have been hurt. I failed to care genuinely because someone had not cared about me. I was saying, *God, you let the girl I loved hurt me, so I don't care who I hurt.*

Don't get me wrong; I was never consciously out to hurt people. However, my self-centeredness made it impossible for me not to hurt other people. I felt little regret if someone else happened to experience the consequences of my actions driven by bitterness. The crazy thing is, through all of this, I was completely justified in my own mind. I thought I could justify my behavior based on my past. I took what had been done to me and dished it out. I never even felt very sorry. In my mind, I hadn't messed up—God had. Now, I believed I was free to do as I wished, and He couldn't say anything about it.

If you do whatever you want long enough, God is going to do one of two things. He is either going to get your attention, or He is going to leave you alone. Pray that it isn't the latter. When God shakes your world, it means He is still drawing you toward Him, and He has not given up on you. When God leaves you alone, that is when you've really got something to worry about. At the time, I had no idea that God was going to shake up my world. Before He did that, however, He was going to let me realize just how pathetic my attempts at righteous living really were. He would let me walk off the deep end as I attempted life on my own. He was going to let me fail.

- *4* -

Freshman Year Freedom

As a recent high school graduate, college orientation proved to be a grand experience. It was the summer before my freshman year of college, and I had traveled two states away to register for classes, meet other freshmen, and experience my first taste of what I like to call *ignorant freedom*. I had never really felt completely free growing up. I had always known rules, and I had accepted them conditionally. If I followed the rules, I believed good things would happen. I had always known what time I was supposed to get home, when I was supposed to go to bed, what I was supposed to eat, what I was supposed to watch or not watch, and what I was allowed to say.

I was certainly cared for and given many opportunities to experience life, but I had never tasted a moment of freedom where I could say, *I can do whatever I want to do right now, and no one is going to stop me.* I had never even realized that that moment existed until orientation weekend. I stood outside the campus student center at 1:00 a.m. talking with some newfound friends about life. I suddenly realized I didn't have to go to bed if I didn't want to. If they were going to stay up talking, then why couldn't I? It was my very first taste of ignorant freedom.

What do I mean by *ignorant freedom*? It's simple. *Ignorant freedom* is freedom that comes from being ignorant. I'm simply referring to a time when I felt unrestricted as a result of obliviousness.

One time, a family was imprisoned inside an enclosed cell. They had been locked away for life, and the only interaction they received with the outside world was the occasional feeding time when food and drink would be dropped through a slot in the wall. In this lonely state of isolation existed a father, a mother, and a young child. Unfortunately for the young child, both parents died soon after the imprisonment and were removed from the cell. The boy, however, remained encaged.

The boy eventually grew up, but he was still locked away and being fed through a slot in the wall. Though he had no education and could not be considered very intelligent by any means, one day, an idea came to him. He thought, *I wonder what is beyond that wall.* In his newfound curiosity, he began to dig away at the wall. He fashioned a pick out of sharp rocks and began to chip at his cage. Years went by, and finally he had created a hole wide enough for his body to squeeze through. In his excitement, he quickly pulled himself through and took his first step outside of his lifelong prison. Peering around, he noticed that he was standing inside another room, similar to his cell but larger. The world that had been his prison for as long as he could remember was enclosed inside another prison cell. He fell down to his knees, lifted his arms and shouted, "Freedom!"

It's incredibly easy to think you are free when you don't understand what freedom really is. It's easy to think you have arrived when you don't know where you are going. What I had broken out into that evening at orientation looked like freedom to me. How was I to know better? In my head, I shouted, *Freedom*, and in my heart I let myself go.

I made incredibly meticulous use of my time during my first semester of college. My attitude, though driven and passionate, was led by a reckless, selfish fastidiousness. I made every effort to do everything and anything I could to live up to my newfound freedom, all the while holding onto the lifelong belief that I was a good person. More importantly, I was holding onto the belief that God *also* still saw me as a good person. I thought God was finally paying me back for being a better person than most people. If you had asked me straight up, I would have denied the idea that I was better than others out of a sense that humility still counted for something. Nonetheless, I intrinsically viewed myself as being better.

As an energetic, hopeful youth, now estranged from my bitterness, I sought friendship in every place available. It was frightfully easy for me to make a throng of friends in a short period of time, and I expelled almost no personal effort. I had a lot going for me. I happened to be a genuinely nice person in my freshman year at a nondenominational Christian college. Taking advantage of my situation, I made friends left and right. I was quickly involved in athletics, art classes, filmmaking groups, dance groups, acting, and video-game-enthusiast groups. Consequently, I began to feel like I had friends around every corner. I considered myself to have taken a wide turn from who I had been back in junior high. I was no longer an introvert. In fact, I had developed into one of the wildest extroverts I knew. I thought, *I've still got God on my side because I've done everything I was supposed to do, and I've stayed away from everything I wasn't supposed to do.*

That was the key. That was my golden ticket. I thought God was blessing me and taking care of me because of what I had done—because of who *I* was. I had no idea that my view of myself was about to change.

The truth about most friends is that they don't stick around after they have had enough of you. Even though it appeared that I had no lack of companions, I still wound up feeling lonely. When all the partying had ended and everyone had split ways for the day, I would find myself still needing people. Often, when I felt alone, I would play video games to distract my mind until someone else came along to help fill my time. I still studied, exercised, and joined in on random activities, but I would inevitably find myself alone. Sometimes I felt like I was on a constant hunt for companionship and excitement.

Like I said earlier, it's incredibly easy to think you are free when you don't understand what freedom really is. It's incredibly easy to think you have arrived when you don't know where you are going. It's incredibly easy to think you have found someone when you don't know who it is you are looking for.

I didn't know who I was looking for. I had everything I could have wanted. I had friends. I had acquaintances. I had exciting adventures. I even had a God who was going to help me out when I really needed Him. I naturally figured, if I felt like something was missing, then I obviously didn't have enough of what I had. I thought, *If I can get more, then I will be satisfied. If I can discover more freedom in life, then I will be complete—then I will be happy.*

With that thought in mind, I added women to the list of things I was chasing. I began going from one girl to the next, convincing myself I was in love, and then suddenly forgetting about her when someone else came along. My ability to justify shuffling through one young lady after another came from the heart of bitterness I had carried since high school. I thought that God was going to bring me someone who would make up for everything I had endured, and I didn't care who I trampled to get to her. I'll be honest. My overarching goal wasn't to treat women with detestation. I just didn't feel any responsibility to genuinely protect someone of the opposite gender—even from myself. In my twisted freshman mind, they seemed like party favors that I would shuffle through until I found the one I wanted.

And I was okay with that.

Women were not enough. My language also began to change. I found no guilt in allowing explicit words and phrases to slip from my lips. It wasn't really too difficult to justify. While before I had viewed cursing and foul jokes as something I would never do, I now saw them as something allowable as long as it wasn't hurting anyone else. As long as it was in a joking manner, I thought I could say anything I felt like saying. More than that, as long as other *Christians* around me were doing it, I could do it too.

Cursing also was not enough. I began watching films and TV shows that I had at one point vowed never to watch. As long as someone else was watching it, I saw nothing wrong with watching even some of the worst films out there—films that should never have been made. As long as I wasn't taking part in the things I saw people on screen doing, I felt like I was okay.

Up to this point, I still could justify everything I was doing. I still thought that my good outweighed my bad. I had failed to notice that as I allowed my moral bounds to stretch, my habits changed as well. I had been taught as a child to eat healthy foods, and now I was eating the worst food I could get my hands on. It all contributed to the sense of "freedom" I thought I was experiencing. I had been taught as a child to go to bed at a decent hour, and now I stayed up all through the night, later fighting to stay awake during daylight hours. I had been taught as a child to be kind and considerate, and I suddenly started hurting people's feelings on purpose. I did it for the thrill of it. I didn't feel like I was losing anything if a couple of my friends didn't like me anymore. I had plenty of friends to spare, so I treated them however I felt like treating them. Even through it all, I justified everything by the fact that I was a child of God. God was going to watch out for me and bless me because of who I was. I had prayed for salvation at a young age and had attempted to stay away from evil, so I believed I was entitled to live my life the way that pleased me the most.

One night, everything changed.

Despite my immense web of friends, a weight of an increasing loneliness joined forces with the predominant idea that I still needed more freedom. So, I began to look at porn. The movies and TV shows that filled my head had helped to grow a desire in me that I thought I would never have. I had always had a normal sexual drive, but I had never thought that I would let it get the best of me. For most of my life, I had prided myself in being *pure*, but now something had changed. After the partying was finished, after the activities were over, and after my friends had gone to bed, I was awake. I fed my eyes with images of nude women who had been paid to expose themselves indecently.

At first, I viewed it as just a slip up. *Everyone makes mistakes*, I reminded myself. *Everyone messes up every once in a while*, I thought. I pushed the thought of it away, hoping that God would just write that one off. I considered that everything good I had ever done would make up for one serious mistake. That wasn't who I was. I was better than that. I was the guy that God was looking out for. I was the guy that God was blessing. In fear of losing my good standing with God, I hoped that one little mistake wouldn't spoil an entire life of blessing.

Then it happened again and again. I went back to it once more, and then once more. It continued to pervade my time. In essence, it pervaded my existence. I continued to evade the idea of it, and I continued to ignore the thought that it would affect me in any real way. It took a while—a longer while than I wish it had—but I eventually began to realize I was not the same person I had once been. I had not just messed up; I was a mess up. I had not simply given in; I had given up. I had not only said yes to something wrong; I had also said no to everything good.

In my desperation, I stayed up later and later, letting the drowsiness cloud my mind. I needed to forget, so I hardly ever slept. I let the lack of sleep and lack of nutrition sedate me into forgetting about what I had been doing just minutes before. I went from one form of entertainment to another, always keeping my mind busy with something new, something fresh, and something that would cause me to forget how rotten I was. The later I stayed up though, the more I gave in. The more I tried to fill my head with other streams of knowledge and amusement, the more they led me straight back to that computer screen—straight back to those websites.

When a man is sliding down a steep muddy slope, the more he struggles to travel back up, the further he can slide down. I was sliding down a slope, I was knee deep in mud, and I had no way of getting out. The only way I was ever going to get out was if someone else would be willing to climb down with a rope and pull me back up. Unfortunately, I had broken my promise to God. I had trusted in the idea that *If I do this, God MUST do that.* I was no longer doing *this* (what God desired me to do). Instead, I was doing something else—something shameful.

In return, I knew that God would also do something else. I hadn't done *this*, so God wouldn't do *that*. God was going to punish me. I knew it. I believed that it was not going to be a light punishment either. I was going to feel it. I had stopped asking God for things. I figured there was no point to it anymore. I figured praying would just make Him angrier. However, because of my great fear of punishment, I eventually decided to ask God for one more thing. One day, I got down on my knees in my room and prayed that God would help me to stop. I asked God to give me the strength to never look at porn again.

God did something amazing that day, but I did not realize that I should have asked for a whole lot more. For some reason I thought freedom from porn was all I needed. That was the day that God gave me the strength to resist the pornography temptation. However, it is sad that I only asked for freedom from one area of sin. What I had not taken into consideration was the fact that my whole life had changed. My standard of morality had descended. It wasn't just porn that had taken a hold of me. It was almost everything I was involved in. I had this small strange hope that, if I did stop, and if I did try to be a good person for a long enough time, God would one day welcome me back to the position I had been in from the start.

After ceasing to view porn, the last thing in the world I wanted was to remind God of my addiction. I wanted Him to see the new me, and I wanted Him to think about me like He once had. The only hope I had now was to lay low—to stay out of God's sights.

What I failed to realize was that even in my horrid, painfully messed up state, God was not done with me. God had a plan for me that I could not imagine. Before I saw that plan, I was first going to get scared. I was going to be confronted by a God who had never messed up, and I would not be able to hide the fact that I was still a mess up.

- 5 -

Sophomore Year: Depression and Sacrifice

I took an inconsequential and comical view of depression until I began to experience it for myself. My only interaction with depression had been stories. I had enjoyed psychological mysteries and cheap thrillers that exploited the hopelessly depressed soul. I saw it as nothing more than entertaining until it hit me in real life. Suddenly, it was different. It wasn't funny. It wasn't amusing. It was simply draining. It was overpowering. The worst part about it was that it continuously reminded me of who I had become.

When I gave up pornography, I put all my hope in the idea that I could make up for my mistakes. If I did enough good for enough time, then maybe someday I could get back to a place of blessing. Sad as it may seem, the more I resisted tempting desires, the more depressed I became. I hated myself. I hated my choice. I began to act more like a good person, but on the inside I felt like a lie. I thought I could change who I was by changing my actions, and I hoped that eventually my feelings would follow. Because of this, I restrained myself from anything that could possibly be considered wrong. I tried to quit cursing. I hardened myself against TV, video games, and movies that contained questionable material. The only thing I could not seem to change was how I treated women. This had become a habit so strong, fueled by bitterness so deep, that it would not budge. Still, I had worse things to worry about.

The more I pulled myself back, the more I fed my depression. I became trapped in an endless cycle of hopelessness. The more I attended church or chapel to feel better, the worse I felt. The harder I tried to forget, the more I discovered that no amount of time would ever fix what I had become. I was like a wounded soldier who thought that layering on more bulletproof vests would fix the bullet hole already in me.

Since time wasn't doing anything to ease my depression, I thought perhaps a lessened sense of reality would. I kept myself awake, only sleeping a few hours a day. I went from one addictive substance to the next. I didn't want to give God more reason to be angry, so I didn't use illegal substances, but I would overuse anything I could get that wasn't illegal. Through all of this, I was still trying to someday arrive at the place I had been.

Then, it finally hit me.

Nothing I was doing was working. No amount of time or obliviousness could change me back into the person I had been, and I began to fear that perhaps what had once existed between God and me was forever lost. At one time, I had considered myself a favorite in His eyes. What was worse was that I still bought into the idea that *If I do this, God must do that.* That was the nastiest feeling I had ever had to face. Time was painting a clear picture in my mind of how badly I had failed at living up to God's expectations. I had failed, and there was no going back. There was no reclaiming of my rights. There was no rewinding of time, and there was no hope left.

I struggled to prevent myself from continuing down the road of moral cause and effect, but there was no stopping the ideas from flowing. I was no longer on the receiving end of things. In my mind, I had transferred to the losing end of the rope. I abruptly saw myself as that guy that God was going to mess with. God would hinder, hurt, and look to ruin me.

I had one chance left—one final stride in a desperate attempt to save myself. If I had spoiled myself and my chances of being in God's favor, then perhaps I could still get out of it all if I could simply stop believing. So, I began to reason in my mind: *Who's to say God exists? If He is just up there to remind us of our mistakes until we die and then throw us into hell, then why does He have to exist? He sounds more like an imagined being constructed by religious groups in order to direct society to their liking. If God isn't real, then I have nothing to worry about. If God isn't real, then I'm still free.*

That is what I chose to believe. For one day, I set out under the speculation that perhaps God was not real. I assumed that my baby brother had died, not because God had let him die, but instead, because there was no God alive to save him. Perhaps I had been mistreated by my "one and only," not because God had let her do what she did, but rather because there was no God to stop her.

For one day, I made the decision to adjust my beliefs in order to fix my mistakes. The day was similar to any other day except for one thing: I had never felt so dirty in my life. It was as if the only real thing about my existence was missing. I felt like I had traded every last decent piece of my heart in for something evil. At the end of the day, I knew that there was no denying it. God was real. I believed God was real, and I would never be able to change that belief.

If you've been reading this and wondering what the point of my story is, don't worry. I'm still getting to it. However, what's more important than the point I want to make is the point God wants to make. As we move forward, I believe God has something that He wants to tell you. I have a simple question for you: are you going to be willing to listen to what He has to say? I'm not talking about *my* words. I'm talking about the constant, loving draw of an all-powerful Creator. I believe you are reading this for a reason, and I hope that you begin to believe it as well. As we have now made it back to the point at which this book started, I'll continue my story.

I stood there that night on my college campus, looking up into the night sky, realizing that I believed in the almighty, all-powerful Creator of the universe, and fear gripped my heart.

The only thing more upsetting to me than the *possibility* of God being real was the realization that I actually *believed* He was real. If God was real, but I had no understanding of His existence, then I seemingly would have had nothing to worry about until I died. I could have gone about my life, pushing myself to find meaning in one activity after another. However, because I truly believed that God was real, I had to acknowledge the fact that I would one day stand before Him face-to-face.

This realization ruined everything.

The reason my understanding of God's existence ruined my plans was because I knew that I had fallen so far short of His standard. I had attempted to wish away the thought of God, but I could not. He had made Himself known through creation, and He had also placed the knowledge of Himself inside of me. I could not ignore it.

I stood there, allowing my thoughts to wander from their normal, binding construct. In my mind, I saw myself gliding along the outskirts of the universe, and I attempted to imagine the extent of its expanse. The stars were brilliant that night. An ever-present God had created an immense universe. In the span of space, He put a world on which a very small person named Troy happened to live. The frightening idea that resulted from my abstract contemplations was that my existence was mostly inconsequential. I could be so easily discarded. God was so big and had so much to deal with, that I felt like my failure at life would ultimately seem insignificant to Him. He might simply squish me and keep going about His business. How could I expect Him to think twice about me? After all, I was made from nothing more than dirt. Emotionally, I was sinking. If I could have only seen what was about to happen, I would have landed on a very different conclusion.

I cried all the time. I slept less than before. Then, one day, I crashed.

Do you ever wish you had a greater purpose? Do you ever wish there was something more than what you could see? If there was, do you wish you could know about it? What I slowly began to acknowledge in my life was a lack of purpose.

Have you ever sat through a boring lecture, counting away the seconds, thinking about what you were going to do after it was over? I felt like I was in the middle of the longest, most boring lecture in history, and I had nothing good to look forward to. Every day, the list of things I needed to restrict myself from grew longer. The crazy thing is that the lecture was being written and executed by my own mind. I was at all times scared—terrified that I was going to mess up and start over again from the beginning. I would stay awake throughout the night, wondering when the lecture was going to end. I constantly wished I had something in which I could hope.

After starting the second semester of my sophomore year, something happened that would change my perspective on purpose forever. I had been so saturated with the idea that I had to redeem myself, that I had not even considered the possibility that God had a bigger plan in mind. I was so overwhelmed with the sinner I had allowed myself to become, that I assumed God was going to be angry with me for a long time. I hoped that someday I would feel like I had a reason for living again. I never suspected that God had in mind a greater reason for me being alive than I could imagine. God knew His plans for me, and He was not about to let me fall into apathy and meaninglessness without a fight. He was about to wake me up.

On a day that I cannot forget, I traveled with six friends out to a lake for an afternoon. We hung out and goofed off for a while before deciding to head back to the school. As we climbed into the vehicle, I persisted in asking to drive. I can't tell you why I experienced such a strong urge to drive, but it was there. So, after some pleading, I was given the keys to my friend's car. I hopped into the driver's seat, excited to be behind the wheel. It didn't seem to bother me that two of my friends were in the trunk area without seatbelts.

We had only traveled a few miles when we came upon a rocky dirt road. I quickly braked at a split in the road and the car persisted before coming to a stop. I don't think I had ever experienced a vehicle slide like that before, so I thought it was fun. I pressed on, taking the rocky path. Crossing a small section of water, we took a sharp right. Driving up the side of a rough slope, I attempted to see what was over the top of the hill.

At the top, I was forced to quickly turn left. As I pulled out of the turn, the car drifted on the gravel road and slid into a tailspin. As the back of the vehicle swung out of control, I tried to quickly correct my mistake. We spun back and forth a few times before I realized that I had only made things worse by fighting the motion of the car.

The SUV dipped into a small gully on the right side of the road, lifted over a small ridge, and smashed through a fence. As we landed, the car began to roll down a hill. We continued to tumble, and I remember noticing a vivid contrast between the blackness of the ground and the brightness of the sky overhead. The images seemed to rotate around the vehicle as it flipped over itself. Later, when we discussed the event, almost everyone else claimed to have blacked out during the crash. I didn't black out. I couldn't. I had nothing to lose. I simply watched it happen, and the only thing that came to my mind were the words, *Well, Jesus, this is it.*

I know now that Jesus was saying, *This isn't it.* He had something better in mind. He had a plan for me. I thought that since I had failed at life, perhaps it was time to give up and go home. However, through this scary situation, Jesus was depositing inside my soul the belief that I had a purpose. It was as if He was communicating, *You don't come home until you finish what I've given you to do.*

Miraculously, the vehicle came to a stop right-side up, and we all crawled out. The crazy thing about that day, was not what had happened though. The crazy thing was what did *not* happen. Seven people went to the lake, and seven people came back from the lake. Only a few minor injuries were sustained. For almost a year, I had thought my life was over, but God reminded me that it wasn't. He showed me that bruises heal. He reminded me that He can mend the cuts and scrapes of life. I did not realize it that day, but He was beginning to stitch me up.

- 6 -

The Beginning of Something New

As my ability to recognize God's hand in my life emerged, I began to believe that God created me for a reason. I wondered how I could discover my purpose. I thought, *God must have saved me for something, but what? If He is planning on using me, why am I still overrun by fear and unrest?* Even though I felt like I could see things differently, nothing in my life had visibly changed. I was still battling the depression. I was still wrapped up in a struggle between right and wrong—and I was still losing. I was still engaged in an endless cycle of spiritual deterioration. I still believed my only hope was to work back toward the self-righteousness I had harbored while growing up. I kept thinking that if I worked hard enough, I could recreate the feeling of justification my good works had at one time provided.

By this point in my story, I hadn't learned much. Because of the circumstances God had allowed to happen, I had discovered a sense of purpose, but that was all I had gathered. However, as I look back, I can now see how God used that internal longing to lead me to Him. It was the idea that my life mattered to God that led me to start reading the Bible. It had been over a year since I had regularly picked up my Bible, but something inside me hoped that I would find the answers to my questions between those thin pages. As I was reading in the New Testament one night, I came across this passage spoken by Jesus:

"Enter through the narrow gate; for the gate is wide and the way is broad that leads to destruction, and there are many who enter through it. For the gate is small and the way is narrow that leads to life, and there are few who find it.

Beware of the false prophets, who come to you in sheep's clothing, but inwardly are ravenous wolves. You will know them by their fruits. Grapes are not gathered from thorn bushes nor figs from thistles, are they? So every good tree bears good fruit, but the bad tree bears bad fruit. A good tree cannot produce bad fruit, nor can a bad tree produce good fruit. Every tree that does not bear good fruit is cut down and thrown into the fire. So then, you will know them by their fruits.

Not everyone who says to Me, 'Lord, Lord,' will enter the kingdom of heaven, but he who does the will of My Father who is in heaven will enter. Many will say to Me on that day, 'Lord, Lord, did we not prophesy in Your name, and in Your name cast out demons, and in Your name perform many miracles?' And then I will declare to them, 'I never knew you; depart from Me, you who practice lawlessness.'"

As I read Matthew 7:13-23, I began to develop a deep fear. I felt afraid for two reasons. The first reason was, when I looked at my life, I could see no good fruit. There simply was none there at all. Instead, my entire existence had revolved around a selfish need to please myself. I could see the obvious difference between what Jesus was saying and what I had been doing.

Good fruit does not necessarily mean doing good things. Good fruit does not simply mean being nice to people or helping people who need help. Good fruit is not just going to church, reading the Bible, or praying. Good fruit is not dressing appropriately, singing the right songs, or acting spiritual. In Mathew chapter 7, Jesus connects good fruit to doing the will of God, and He shows that it is impossible to do the will of God if you do not truly know Him. You can go around doing good all day, but if you do not truly know God, then what you have done will have no impact on your eternity.

As I examined the passage from Matthew, I realized that some of the people doing things for God did not actually know Him. They had been involved in God's work, but they did not have a relationship with God's Son. It made me seriously consider my Christian life growing up. I had done a lot of good works, but I could see little or no relationship behind my actions. Instead, duty and reward had motivated me.

The second reason I felt scared was this: Jesus said to "enter through the narrow gate." Why did He say this? He said it because those who do not enter through the narrow gate will never enter at all. Those who do not enter through the gate that Jesus is talking about will never see the kingdom of heaven. The reason this realization scared me so much is because I was doing the same things everyone else was doing. I was living the same way that almost every other good Christian I knew was living. I was surrounded by people who viewed God the same way I did.

You might say, *It's good to be surrounded by other Christians.* When Jesus said that people would say, "Lord, Lord," He was not talking about unbelievers. He was talking about Christians. He was talking about people who grew up in church—people who grew up knowing about Him, talking about Him, and even claiming to follow Him. He was talking about so-called believers who end up missing the narrow gate. He was talking about people who prayed a prayer but never entered into a relationship. He was talking about people who knew what it meant to look like a Christian but didn't know what it meant to be in Christ. The unbelievers definitely aren't going to be standing there saying, "Jesus, did we not do all these things in your name?" Some who considered themselves Christians are going to be saying that.

This realization thoroughly scared me. It scared me so badly that I decided I needed to do something about it. That night, I made the decision I thought I had made years earlier in children's church, and again in youth group when I went up front and said that I would follow Christ. That night, I truly decided to follow Him, and my life has never been the same.

You might say, *But we no longer have to be scared of God because of what Jesus did on the cross.* Listen to the words of Jesus in Matthew 10:28:

> *"Do not fear those who kill the body but are unable to kill the soul; but rather fear Him who is able to destroy both soul and body in hell."*

Jesus Himself told us to fear God. Why? Until we develop a healthy fear of God, rooted in the fact that He is both completely just and fully loving, we will never reach out and take hold of the truth. Until we understand the wrath our sin put us under, we will never realize our great need for the real, living Savior who took the wrath upon Himself. Unless we develop the fear of the Lord the Bible talks about (Proverbs 9:10), we will simply continue living like everyone else, justifying our actions by what we see other Christians or good people doing. If we don't approach God with an understanding of the consequences of sin, we'll never be any closer to walking on the narrow path Jesus talks about.

When I made a decision that I was going to enter through the narrow gate, I also committed my steps to the narrow path. It's more than just making a commitment, though. That night when I committed my life to the Lord, I still had a strong sense of duty and performance leading my beliefs. Because of the fear of the Lord, I had decided to live completely for Jesus, and I assumed that meant a life of grueling work for His kingdom. I still considered my works of value. I had little knowledge of how good the gospel really is.

If my words have been depressing you, I want you to know that it gets so much better. What Jesus did for us on the cross is so much better than just giving us a reason to work harder. He did so much more than simply provide a motivation for a deeper commitment. This was something I still needed to learn, but I had made a decision to give my life to Him, and that was a good first step.

When we become believers, we are taken from darkness to light. When we allow Christ to live in us, we live in such a way that we shine light into a dark place. Jesus tells us that the darkness hates the light (see John 3:19-21), but that should not stop us from shining. Instead, because of the intensity of the light inside us, we ought to shine all the more. Those who are walking in darkness do not like to be told that there is light out there, because walking into light means leaving the dark deeds behind. In order to find the truth, one has to accept that there only is one truth.

Jesus Christ is the way, the truth, and the life (John 14:6). You may have heard that a million times, but it still needs to be said because it is still the truth. As an imperfect human, I sometimes listen to my heart rather than the Word of God. My heart often follows the way of the old man, being satisfied with living on the fence between the shadow and the sun. If the heart is above all deceitful (Jeremiah 17:9), then we need to stop listening to our hearts and begin listening to the truth, which only comes from God.

As I began allowing the light of God's Word to shine into my heart, revealing the darkness that had long abided there, I realized how much change needed to happen. I looked at my life, and I could see that God had a major job on His hands. I did not want to be one of the "followers" who ended up saying "Lord, Lord." I worried about my salvation. I wondered how I could be certain that I was on my way to heaven. Even after committing my life to Jesus, I still feared that my commitment would not be enough. I could not see that I was still misinterpreting the meaning behind Jesus being the only way to the Father.

Even in my fear and confusion, I knew that salvation was obtained through Jesus. I had read that Jesus was the only way, and so I continued to run to Him. I didn't go attend a church service and walk down front. I didn't join a small group or a Bible study. Those things are good, but I had done all of that before. I was still bound by fear and condemnation. I was still not free. I had attempted to live a Christian life, I had messed up, and now I knew that the only thing that could set me free was Jesus Christ. The craziest part of my story may be the fact that I had been attending church my whole life, and yet I had still not found Jesus. I had learned a lot about Him, and I had talked about Him, but I had never initiated a relationship with Him.

I'm going to ask you a question. It may be a difficult question because it may mean a re-evaluation of the motivation behind your Christian life. It could mean examining your beliefs and not liking the outcome. The question is this: If every person in the Bible who truly found Jesus Christ found a life-altering truth, then have you truly found Jesus Christ? Have you truly been changed? Has the gospel radicalized your life at all? Or, similar to my college-aged self, are you just doing the Christian thing, hoping not to sin as much as you have before? I know these are strong words. Take heart, because there is good news coming.

When I took a long look at my life, I saw no change. I saw no truth that set me free. All I saw was a truth that engrossed me in an ocean of guilt and worthless hopes. All I saw was a young man who desired to be like Christ but knew he never could. The harder I tried, the quicker I had to start over at the beginning. Part of me thought that this was just the way the Christian life was meant to be lived, but I also did not want to give up. I needed to know real freedom.

If you read Acts chapter 10, you will hear about a man named Cornelius that feared God and prayed to Him continually. He was also known for his charitable giving. One day, God sent an angel to him telling him to invite Peter to come visit him. Cornelius was a Gentile, and Peter would not have normally agreed to visit with Gentiles. However, God was working it out. As Cornelius' men were on their way, Peter was given a vision telling him that he should preach to Gentiles as well as Jews. At the end of the vision he was specifically told to go with Cornelius' men when they asked. He went to Cornelius and preached the gospel of Jesus Christ to Cornelius and his household. The Bible says that the Holy Spirit fell on everyone who heard the message of the gospel.

Here was a man who did not know God and yet did the work of God, and so God found a way to save him. He sought after God even though he did not understand the gospel. God sent Peter to proclaim the gospel to him so that he and his household might know Jesus Christ. If a man who did not yet know Christ did the work of the Lord, why is it then that we who claim to know Jesus are sometimes still living for ourselves? Cornelius was seeking the heart of God. Are we truly seeking God's heart? This question should put a healthy fear of God in us. Why is it that we who claim to be followers of Christ so often make our decisions based on what the culture is saying instead of what Jesus is saying? Is it possible that we have slapped the title of Christian on ourselves and then headed in our own direction?

I believe that the Christian church needs to stop relating salvation so much to an experience and begin to relate it more to a Person. Instead of asking, "Have you been saved?" it may be more beneficial to ask, "Do you know Jesus?" According to Jesus in Matthew 7, there is no salvation apart from knowing Him. Am I rejecting the idea of *once saved always saved?* Not necessarily. I am saying that what a great majority of people believed to be an experience where they gave their life to Jesus Christ was simply an experience where they prayed a prayer and experienced no change. I'm not saying that you can lose your salvation. What I'm saying is that many people who think they are saved—aren't.

You might be thinking, *How can you say that? You can't judge people's hearts! Only God can do that.* And you would be right to say that. I can't judge people's hearts, and I'm not trying to. Please don't think that I'm saying this because I've looked around and decided that some people aren't really saved. The only heart I can examine is my own. I am simply repeating what Jesus has already said. A lot of people who believe themselves to be on the right path are going to end up saying, "Lord, Lord," and Jesus is going to say, "I never knew you." I'm only saying it because Jesus said it. I'm saying it because I love you, and I want you to get it. Being a follower of Christ does not have to do with simply going down front and praying a prayer. It has to do with truly *knowing* Christ.

I am not trying to make you feel guilty so that you will begin to do what is right. You may already have a genuine, growing relationship with Jesus. If so, I could not be happier for you. If you do not, please don't think that I'm trying to judge you. I did not write this book because I have any right to judge. I wrote this book because I was in constant fear of judgment, and God removed that fear. If you're reading my story and you feel like you're in a similar position, my heart is that you experience the same life-giving freedom that I have experienced. Before I could experience freedom, something specific had to happen, and that moment in my story is coming up.

While I'm not trying to put guilt on you, I am attempting to make you step back and see the truth of the situation. Are you really following Christ? Are you simply living life, wondering what heaven is going to be like? The cool thing about having a deep relationship with Jesus is that we already partially know what heaven is going to be like because we already know the One who we will commune with when we arrive. If you aren't walking with Jesus right now, there is hope. There is *so* much hope for you. Please don't let your Christian walk be all about watching Christian videos, listening to worship music, or attending church.

What is so bad with the Christian church? I am not saying that church is a bad thing. Church was planned by God and initiated by Jesus Himself. But as Christians, I believe we have sinned through omission more than commission. The life-changing gospel of Jesus should produce in us a radical, unstoppable love for people, and yet where is this radical love being displayed in the Christian church? I'm not saying that all churches are dead, but it's not hard to see that some are.

Let me give you an example of what I'm talking about. Now, I need to warn you that I'm about to say some direct words about abortion. Before you read them, I need you to know that I am not condemning you if you have had an abortion, considered having an abortion, or have encouraged someone else to have an abortion. I believe that abortion is wrong. God talks about knowing us while we were still in our mother's womb (Jeremiah 1:5), and I believe that classifies babies of any age as human beings. However, I also believe that Jesus can forgive abortion the same way that He can forgive any sin. If you've been involved in having an abortion, please know that God does not want you to live in shame or guilt. In fact, He still loves you perfectly. The Bible tells us that love covers a multitude of sins (1 Peter 4:8). That means that no matter what sin you or I have committed, God's love can still cover us. Even better, He wants to set us free today if we will trust in the finished work of Jesus on the cross.

With that being said, I am going to talk about abortion. The number of abortions that occur every day should shock us as the body of Christ, not cause us to shut down. Yet some of us in the Christian church have either said, "Well, it's probably okay," or we have simply ignored it. I'm not saying that everyone has done this, but some of us have. There are those of us Christians who have done the same thing with abortion that we have done with our own lives: we have just kept ignoring the issue, all the time thinking that God is on our side.

In the same way whites enslaved blacks during the beginning of The United States, this generation has had the right to enslave infants. Parents have the right to end the life of their own unborn child the same way a white slave owner had the right to kill their black slave. Slavery was an atrocity. How can we view abortion any differently? Some of those in the Christian church were standing by and watching it happen then. Where is the radical love of the Christian church that should be standing up to do something about it now?

Like I said, please do not feel any condemnation if you have had an abortion. Jesus can forgive and redeem you right now. There is hope. There is hope because God still loves you perfectly. You have not fallen too far to be forgiven. Abortion is like any other sin; you can be forgiven and set free by believing that Jesus has paid the full price for your sins. God's Word even tells us that love keeps no record of wrongs (1 Corinthians 13:4-7). Thank God that He has kept no record of my wrongs, because my own sin has been no less sinful than anyone else's.

I personally know someone who had six abortions, and she later gave her life to the Lord. Since then, she has birthed seven healthy children, and she has raised them all to follow Christ. I'm telling you that Jesus can redeem.

My point is that there are many problems in the world today that need to be met with the radical, life-altering love of Christ. If we are being led by the Spirit of God, then we are going to be compelled to do something. When we ignore the problem and ignore our own consciences, we are ignoring the One that put our consciences in place. Some of us get as far away from His presence as possible, while still going to church every Sunday. How can we assume that God is for us if we are turning our noses up to the injustices of society? God instructed us to take care of the widows and orphans, and there is no child more orphaned than the one who is being stripped of their life before they even leave the womb.

Maybe some of us have not ignored it completely, but instead we have thought, *There isn't anything I can do about it.* The Word of God says differently. God says that we can do all things through Christ who strengthens us (Philippians 4:13). God says that if He is for us, who can be against us (Romans 8:31)? He says that we are more than conquerors through Him who loves us (Romans 8:37). The issue is not that we haven't heard these verses. The issue is that we have trouble believing them. Our actions do not save us, but they do reveal what is inside us. If a radical love is not pouring out of us for others, then how can we say that we have been changed by a radical gospel?

I know the previous several paragraphs were difficult to swallow, but I had a reason for writing them. Please believe me that I'm not trying to make you feel bad. I'm trying to help you examine the fruit in your life. God has given us the ability to sense right and wrong. If we thought there was nothing wrong with the way things are going in society, then our consciences would not be working. Similarly, if we are not responding to the injustices around us in love, then it's possible that we are not allowing His Spirit to lead us. The Bible tells us that no one can come to Jesus unless God draws that person to Him (John 6:44). The issue is not that God has left us alone. The issue is that some of us have been ignoring His calling on our hearts. We have allowed what the world thinks about something to overrule what God thinks about it.

The reason I've been side-tracking is because I wanted to paint a picture of what I had done in my own life. As I looked at myself in a spiritual mirror, I knew that the only hope I had was Jesus Christ. I could plainly see that my actions were not being motivated by the love of God, and I sensed that I was not allowing

Him to lead me. A choice sat before me: I could either continue to ignore the issue, or I could make a change. The more I read the gospel, the clearer it became to me that Jesus was my only chance at making a change.

Be careful what you feed your children. If you have young children either now or in the future, what you feed them will greatly influence the person they become. My mother used to play a cassette tape for me when I was a young boy. I would listen to this tape when I had trouble falling asleep, and the lyrics of one of the songs that played come straight from a verse in the Bible. The song went like this: *When you seek Me you'll find Me, when you seek Me with all your heart.* It was a direct quote of Jeremiah 29:13. In my hour of desperation, the tune came back to me. I had committed my life to Jesus because I was ashamed of what I had become. I was seeking God because I was terrified of what would happen to me if I did not. As I began to pray one night, the words of the children's song came back.

My mom had made sure that I had heard the Word, and it came back to me when I needed it. I listened to the tune in my mind, letting the Word saturate my heart. I believed that God existed, and I believed that the Bible was the Word of God. So I decided that I could believe that the verse was true. As I began to believe it, I did what God said. I sought Him, and I decided that I was going to seek Him with all my heart. Emotionally, I was still falling apart, so I just let it all fall in front of Him. I wasn't sure how to seek Him because I don't think I had ever truly sought Him with all my heart. I didn't know what it meant to find Him because I never really had. I wasn't sure what I was getting myself into. I simply laid down on the common room floor of my dorm suite and began to pray.

It was late at night, so nobody else was in the room. I put my face to the floor and said, "God, if You are real, I want to know You. If You are real, I want to experience You. I want to know You the way your Word says I can know You. I want to know You the way I've heard all my life but never really experienced." Then, I said something that took faith. It meant that I would be giving up my own desires for His. I said, "God, I want you to fill me with your Holy Spirit the same way you filled all those guys in the New Testament. I'm tired of faking it, Lord. I'm tired of sitting here in my own mess, wishing I had never done what I did. I'm done with dreaming about the way things used to be. I want what You have promised to those who find You."

God didn't say the Christian life would always be comfortable, but He did say that we would find Him if we sought Him with all our hearts. I began to realize that seeking God with my whole heart would require me to seek Him for who He was instead of who I wanted Him to be. It meant trusting Him to change my desires because I knew that I could not please Him on my own.

In the end, I made a choice to simply believe. I began to realize that if God really was real, and I had faith to believe Him, then there should have been nothing to stop me from doing everything He had called me to do. Looking back, I can testify to that truth. When you really believe that God is who He says He is, your life will never be the same. If we believe God's Word is actually true, then we ought to be lining up our thinking with His Word on every occasion. As I lay on that dorm floor, that is exactly what I chose to do. God asked for my whole heart, so I gave it the best way I knew how.

I lay down before Him and prayed, and then I waited. As the days passed, I continued to wait. Weeks went by, and I simply read His Word, prayed, and waited. As I went through my days accomplishing menial tasks, I concentrated on Him. At first, I did not notice much change, but I did not allow myself to give up hope that God was actually going to do something. There were times when I wanted to doubt, and I was tempted to believe that I was wasting my time. However, I began to understand that the more I waited on God, the more I was encouraged to continue seeking Him. Isaiah 40:31 confirms this when it says:

"Yet those who wait for the Lord will gain new strength; they will mount up with wings like eagles, they will run and not get tired, they will walk and not become weary."

Waiting was a process, and it still is to this day. The need to wait on God never seems to cease, but then comes the strength. So, I kept it up. I continued to wait because I believed that God was going to do something.

This story may help you understand my reasoning behind waiting so long. One day, a very religious man visited a prophet and asked him to pray that God would give him an answer to a difficult situation. The prophet agreed, and so the religious man left. When the religious man returned, the prophet said, "God has told me that He will visit you tonight and give you the answer you seek."

In excitement, the very religious man vowed to stay up all night and wait for God. He waited for a few hours, but then drowsiness kicked in. He could not allow himself to fall asleep though, so he bore the discomfort and kept himself awake, continuing to wait for God to show up.

The hours passed, and finally the very religious man gave up. He went straight over to the place where the prophet lived and pounded on his door. When the prophet answered the door, the very religious man exclaimed furiously, "You are no prophet! You said that if I waited all night, God would come and answer me. I have waited and waited, and He never showed up."

The prophet answered calmly, "You haven't seen Him because you did not really believe that He was going to show up."

The religious man was furious. "Of course I believed," he answered.

"Did you really believe?" asked the prophet. "The night is almost over, but it is not morning yet. If you had really believed God was going to show up, you would still be there waiting."

God has already spoken a Word to us. He has given us the Bible, yet we sometimes pick and choose what we want to believe from His Word. When we do this, we're going to end up like the religious man who felt let down by God. If we want God to be at work in our lives, then we need to take His Word seriously. We need to choose to read it and believe it for what it really says, not for what we want it to say.

As Christians, it's easy to come up with excuses to not wait on God. We can take every opportunity to try to solve things on our own, and then we get mad when God doesn't do anything on our behalf. We frustrate ourselves with the notion that God has let us down. The truth is that we sell ourselves short. One reason we have not waited on God is because we did not believe that He was going to do anything in the first place. When we do this, we set our unbelief above the Word of God and above His truth.

Some of us have shaken our fists at God thinking, *You didn't do this, so I don't have to do that.* We get away with having the appearance of waiting by singing songs at church, but how often do we just let the noise drown out His Spirit? We appear to wait by reading our Bibles occasionally, measuring our progress by the number of chapters read instead of by how much we heard from God. When we are doing godly things in an attitude of unbelief, we're not really walking in faith. I know that probably sounds harsh, but please understand that I'm writing about what I myself have done. I do not know every person's heart—I don't know *your* heart. I can only talk about what I have witnessed in my own life.

God has a bigger agenda, however. He has a good plan in mind, even when I choose not to believe Him. When all is said and done, His plan is going to be fulfilled, and you and I are able to get in on it if we want to. Even if we reject His plans, they will still be fulfilled. History is still heading in the same direction that God has revealed in His Word, and I pray that we are not the ones who end up saying, "Lord, Lord."

This thought may raise a question in your mind: *How can I be sure of my salvation? Especially if I feel like I've done too much, or I've fallen too far—is there a way to be sure?* There is a way to be certain, and I intend to explain how and why we can be certain as I continue telling my story.

Because I chose to believe what He had said in His Word, I made the decision to wait on God. Waiting was all I knew to do. I understood that I needed Jesus, and I knew that He had asked for my heart—my whole heart.

Then, one night, while I lay before Him, God did something.

- 7 -

Oh! God Wasn't Kidding. He is Father, Son, and Holy Spirit

I lay there, waiting on Him. I didn't know what I was waiting for; I just knew that I was waiting on God in response to His words in Jeremiah. After reading about the experiences of the New Testament believers, I had also asked Him to fill me with the Holy Spirit, and I believed that He would.

Suddenly, radiating from the stillness, I heard a voice. I had assumed that Biblical characters had always heard these loud, booming voices. However, the voice I heard was not loud; it resembled a whisper. It also wasn't fierce, like I had feared God's voice would be. It was gentle—peaceful, and kind. As the Holy Spirit began to speak to my heart, He said some of the most incredible things I had heard in my life. He said, *Fear not, for I am with you. I have made you and I have called you. I have set you on high because I love you. When you were in trouble, I came to you. I did not stop until I had redeemed my chosen ones. I have put my Spirit upon you for I have called you by name. Do not be afraid, and do not worry.*

What on earth? I could hardly believe what I had heard. The God of the universe had just taken the time to speak to me, and He was not reminding me of my failure. He was not listing His disappointments in me. He was reminding me of how passionately He loved me.

As soon the voice stopped speaking, I got up and ran out of the common room of my suite. I ran into the atrium of my dorm and began to do jumping jacks, trying to release some of the adrenaline. I was utterly shocked. Though I had believed God was going to do something, I was still stunned when He did. After a few more jumping jacks, I ran back into my suite and lay down once more.

I lay there again, waiting on God—waiting on His Spirit. Then, He began to speak to me in a gentle whisper again. He said, *I have called you for a purpose. You don't know what it is right now, but I know it. I know it, and I know you. I have seen you from afar, searching for Me, trying to find Me, so I called to you, and I have saved you. So stop being afraid of all this. All this stuff that you think is too much—it is nothing. I am sufficient for you. I will be there for you when no one else will, holding you with My righteous right hand.*

When the voice of God speaks to you, it isn't like an ordinary voice. It is not audibly heard, as one would hear the voice of a friend. Rather, it closer resembles a change of heart. It is that moment when you cease listening to your own desires, and you allow God to speak truth to your spirit. You hear words as if they were coming from your heart, yet you know that they originate from someplace much further, and much greater. As I lay there, I felt as if my soul were a well through which the voice of God had been echoing for eternity, and the words had finally reached me at the bottom.

There is no perfect way to explain the voice of God because it is unlike anything I have ever experienced. As He continued to encourage me, I simply lay there, taking it all in. I let His words and His presence to change me. Paul says in 1 Corinthians 6:19, "Or do you not know that your body is a temple of the Holy Spirit who is in you, whom you have from God, and that you are not your own?" My body had suddenly been changed. I knew that it was no longer a place for me to dwell in sin, seeking peace and yet finding none. It was now a place for God to work, for God to move, and for God to speak.

Jesus says it like this in John 14:16-17:

"I will ask the Father, and He will give you another Helper, that He may be with you forever; that is the Spirit of truth, whom the world cannot receive, because it does not see Him or know Him, but you know Him because He abides with you and will be in you."

He later says in John 14:23:

"...If anyone loves Me, he will keep my word; and my Father will love him, and We will come to him and make Our abode with him."

You might be thinking, *I believe that the Holy Spirit is real, but what is your biblical backing for all this "voice of God" stuff?* If so, I encourage you to search the Word of God for yourself, asking God to reveal how the Holy Spirit is meant to be working in our lives. However, you can probably guess that I too had questions after hearing His voice for the first time, and so I began to read about the Holy Spirit myself. In John 14:25-26, Jesus says:

"These things I have spoken to you while abiding with you. But the Helper, the Holy Spirit, whom the Father will send in My name, He will teach you all things, and bring to your remembrance all that I have said to you."

Paul says this in 1 Corinthians 2:16:

"For who has known the mind of the Lord that he may instruct him? But we have the mind of Christ."

Jesus says in Matthew 22:43:

"How is it then that David, speaking by the Spirit..." (NIV)

Also, when Elijah heard the voice of God on the mountain, He heard God's Spirit as a soft, still voice. 1 Kings 19:12 says:

"After the earthquake came a fire, but the Lord was not in the fire. And after the fire came a gentle whisper."

I had taken so much time trying to get on God's good side, but I had failed to find Him. I had failed to truly find Him because I had not sought after Him with my whole heart. I did not seek after Him with my whole heart because I did not believe He would respond. It's not because I had never heard of the love and grace of God. I just did not believe that the love and grace of God were big enough to cover my mess. When I finally began to believe that God was going to do what He said He was going to do, I found Him. I found an intimate, personal, friendship with Jesus through the Holy Spirit. When I finally found Him, I was set free.

Before I move forward, I need to make something clear. The words that the Holy Spirit has spoken to me are not equal to the Bible. They are not the written Word of God, so please don't make them into more than what they are. The Bible is God's written Word to us, but the Holy Spirit has the ability to speak revealed words as well. Keep in mind, the words I received from the Holy Spirit were meant as specific encouragements to me personally. Does that mean you can't be encouraged by them? No. I believe that you can. However, I don't believe God wants you to always hear from Him through a third party. I believe He desires to speak to you Himself. If you wish to hear from God, the best place to start is by reading His Word. If you examine what He said to me that night in my dorm, you'll notice that most of what He said can be traced directly back to different Scriptures. Ask Him to make His Word come alive to you, and I believe that He will.

After being filled with the Spirit, I sought Him every day, and I began to constantly experience the peace of God. His Spirit walked with me, and it seemed like no external circumstance could take His peace from me. When someone would say, "Troy, we've still got hours of work left on this huge class project that we've been up all night working on. We're not going to finish in time." I would simply smile and say, "Don't worry. We've got it." Something inside me had changed. A peace was radiating from inside me that didn't make any sense to my natural mind. I knew we had it because I knew that God had it. When I would hear bad news, excitement welled up inside of me. Instead of fearing what I heard, I now awaited what God was going to do, knowing that He really did have my back.

All my life, I had thought God had my back. All my life, I had lived with relative peace, thinking that God was going to be with me as long as I didn't mess up. When I eventually recognized my sin, I thought I had lost Him. I thought He hated me and that stole my peace. When I truly found Him, He provided all the peace I would ever need. If I faced a horrible situation before, it meant to me that God had forgotten about me. Now I understood that God would walk with me right through the middle of disaster, and He would give me unshakable peace. The Apostle Paul calls it peace that surpasses all understanding (Philippians 4:7).

More than simply having peace, I also began to notice the Lord's favor. I know it sounds crazy, but my schoolwork seemed to complete itself. I never ran out of inspiration, and I never ran out of fuel. My entire attitude toward life had changed: God was with me, so who could be against me? If I sat down to write a paper, ideas would come to me in an instant. If I sat down to work on an art project, inspiration would flow as if a chamber orchestra of raw talent was conducting itself in my mind. I'm not saying that I was suddenly perfect at everything or that I didn't have to work hard. However, I witnessed an obvious difference between my work before and after being filled with the Spirit. The only times I would face difficulty in school was when I would look at a project and think, *Maybe I can't really do this.* When I began to doubt, I was not doubting my own ability, but the ability of the One who was within me. When I stopped everything, waited on God, and sought His face, everything would change—every time. People even began to ask me why I had such confidence during difficult situations. I would simply respond, "I know that God is with me."

When you begin to experience the presence of Jesus Christ through the Holy Spirit, your days always seem to be long enough. There is always enough time. There is always enough money. There is always enough provision. Philippians 4:19 states:

"And my God will supply all your needs according to His riches in glory in Christ Jesus."

I had known this verse for years, but I had never understood that to have your needs met means to be in Christ Jesus. It means to be in Him who is the provider. When we look at God and say, "There isn't enough," God might just look at us and say something like, "You're telling Me there isn't enough of something I made out of nothing?" When you abide in Christ, and He abides in you, it's not rare that you witness the power of God. You begin to understand that no matter how bad things get, no matter how messed up things seem, and no matter how little there seems to be, God is in control. With an all-powerful God as your provider, there is no lack. I'm not just talking about financial or material provision either. With God, there is always peace, hope, joy, grace, and love.

We spend so much time seeking comfort instead of seeking the Comforter, that we often forget the true provision of God. The greatest provision He gives us is life and life to the full (John 10:10). I tried ardently to free myself of my shame, but I was only free when I found Him who became our freedom. If there is a lack—whether it be temporal or eternal in nature—Jesus is the answer. We often joke that the answer to every question in Sunday School is Jesus. However, if you really step back and look at it, you will find that the answer to everything you face is always and entirely Jesus Christ.

You may think, *Well, my life is pretty comfortable. I think I've got all the God I need right now.* Just because your life is comfortable does not mean you have found God. In fact, the devil may want you to be comfortable. He is okay with you being surrounded by as many little comforts as you can imagine, because he knows it's easy to trust in comforts instead of trusting in God. If he can get you comfortable enough, you won't have any need for someone to save you. If he can get you seeking enough of something else, you will feel like you don't need to seek God.

America is a society of comfort, and so are many other places. When we have a problem, we take something to comfort ourselves, we drink something to comfort ourselves, we eat something to comfort ourselves, or we watch something to comfort ourselves. The truth is that God wants to comfort us through the Holy Spirit, but we in our own comforts have missed His true freedom. If we continue to ignore His call on our lives, we will always need those temporary comforts. I'm not saying that all earthly comforts are intrinsically bad, but they will never truly fulfill us. Lasting, fulfilling comfort only comes from walking in the Spirit. In John 16:7, Jesus says:

"Nevertheless I tell you the truth; it is expedient for you that I go away: for if I go not away, the Comforter will not come unto you; but if I depart, I will send him unto you." (KJV)

Jesus has promised that the Holy Spirit will be our Comforter. Why don't we just let God do what God is good at, instead of taking everything upon ourselves? When we take our eyes off of the draws of life, and put them on Him, He gives us true, lasting comfort.

- *8* -

Turning Everything Upside Down

If you read about Daniel in the Old Testament, you'll see that he was a man who sought God. He sought God, not only during the normal seasons of life, but also when everything was falling apart. The kingdom of Babylon attempted to strip the national customs and beliefs from Daniel and his peers. As they were being trained in the ways of Babylon, the young Jewish men probably felt like God would understand if they just went along with the instructions of their captors. The Law of God prohibited the Israelites from eating certain foods, but when they were taken captive and brought to Babylon, they were forced to eat from a sinful menu. They were told to do the things God had commanded them not to do. Instead of using their captivity as an excuse to get away with something, Daniel took it as an opportunity to seek his God. Daniel 1:5 says:

> *"The king appointed for them a daily ration from the king's choice food and from the wine which he drank, and appointed that they should be educated three years, at the end of which they were to enter the king's personal service."*

The king's instructions were not an option. The young men were ordered to eat what the king had set before them, and they could expect serious consequences for disobeying. Something about Daniel, though, fed his courage. Something allotted him the boldness to stand up against the ruling of *a* king and follow the ruling of *the* King. Daniel's confidence came from the fact that he walked with God. If we jump ahead to Daniel 6:10, we see that Daniel was a man who sought after His God every day. We also see his devotion to God.

> *"Now when Daniel knew that the document was signed, he entered his house (now in his roof chamber he had windows open toward Jerusalem); and he continued kneeling on his knees three times a day, praying and giving thanks before his God, as he had been doing previously."*

This verse refers to another event in Daniel's life, and I included it because it lets us know that Daniel went after God every day. Seeking God was part of his life—it was his first priority. In fact, Daniel did this directly after the king passed a decree forbidding anyone from praying to God. Daniel's devotion to God is obvious because he was defying the law of the land, but even more so because he was doing it openly. During this time, he regularly opened his windows while praying, allowing the authorities to witness His loyalty to the Lord.

When Daniel was instructed to eat the foods that were set before him, we see a similar reaction. In boldness, he went to the chief official and asked for a change.

> *"But Daniel made up his mind that he would not defile himself with the king's choice food or with the wine which he drank; so he sought permission from the commander of the officials that he might not defile himself."*

Daniel 1:8

What comes next raises my interest. Let's look at verses 9 and 10:

> *"Now God granted Daniel favor and compassion in the sight of the commander of the officials, and the commander of the officials said*

to Daniel, 'I am afraid of my lord the king, who has appointed your food and your drink; for why should he see your faces looking more haggard than the youths who are your own age? Then you would make me forfeit my head to the king.'"

The chief official knew what he was talking about. There were heavy stakes involved. What I think some of us fail to see in this story is that Daniel knew the stakes as well. He went to the chief official, someone who probably had direct authority over Daniel's life, and he asked him to defy the king's command. That took guts. Daniel was basically risking his life. He was putting God's laws above his own wellbeing—his own survival.

The radical part of the story occurs in verse 9, where it says, "Now God granted Daniel favor and compassion in the sight of the commander…" Daniel's story is amazing because God actually had Daniel's back. Daniel stepped out in faith, and God did something. God worked on his behalf. When I read this, I'm left with a question: *Why did God work on his behalf?* One obvious assumption is to say that it was because Daniel lived righteously. However, I want to challenge this notion. The Bible is full of people who thought they were doing the right thing and yet found God working against them. The Pharisees are one of the best examples of a group of people who followed the Law down to the very letter. They did everything right, or so they thought. For some reason they failed to find favor with God.

Remember what Jesus says about the Pharisees in Luke. In chapter 11 verse 42 He says:

"But woe to you Pharisees! For you pay tithe of mint and rue and every kind of garden herb, and yet disregard justice and the love of God; but these are the things you should have done without neglecting the others."

Jesus uses some fairly harsh words against the Pharisees. His frustration is justified too because the Pharisees did everything they were "supposed" to do, and yet they still failed to find God. If you have attended church for any amount of time, you've probably heard the common warning against being like the Pharisees. A strangely sad characteristic about the Pharisees, however, is that they were referred to as "blind guides." So, if one is like a Pharisee, then one would not be able to rectify one's self, because they could not see who they really were. If you are like the Pharisees, you probably won't even know it unless the Spirit of God reveals it to you. Here's the key to freedom: God can reveal the motives of our hearts that are unpleasing to Him, if we ask.

Perhaps you've had a love for following the Law without a genuine love for God. Maybe you've simply never realized what it means to truly love God. Could you be in the camp of people that have had a church experience but have never experienced the power and loving mercies of God? We can look around and see what everyone else is doing and think, *This is the way Christianity is meant to be.* Have we really asked God what His version of Christianity looks like? The Pharisees had missed it, but Jesus showed up having a real connection to God.

Here's the truth I want you to see: if a part of the Christian church has no connection with the real, living God, then they've missed it. I'm not passing judgment on specific groups; I'm telling you about the type of Christianity that I became comfortable living with. It's easy to grow so comfortable with the way things are that we miss out on what God really intends for our lives. *If God really meant more for me, then how come He put me where He did?* I believe you are where you are for a specific purpose. I believe that God put this book in your hands for a reason—the same way He allowed you to go through the circumstances you've gone through for a reason. It may be that the Holy Spirit is asking you to make a choice. It may be now that blinders are being removed from your eyes. Right now, you have an opportunity. Right now, you have a choice.

When Daniel and his friends looked around at what the other young men were doing, they could have thought, *This is all there is so we should just accept it.* Instead, Daniel stood up boldly and said, *God has a better plan than this in mind.* Where did his boldness come from? It wasn't a product of his learned adherence to the rules. Daniel's boldness came directly from God. His courage came directly from the God he knew. Daniel used a trial as an opportunity to seek God's will. Daniel was not working *for* himself and he wasn't walking *by* himself. Daniel was putting everything he had on the line. He was giving his entire being toward the work that God had called him to do, and we see that God was with Him.

In Matthew 22:37, Jesus says:

"...love the Lord your God with all your heart, and with all your soul, and with all your mind."

We aren't called to love God with our money. We aren't called to love God with our time, what we eat or drink, how often we go to church, or how many songs we sing. Instead, we are called to love God with everything we have. The fact that God is perfect and holds a perfect standard for us is the very reason I stood under the stars that night, looking up at the sky in fear. When I realized that God deserved and desired to have every part of me, I freaked out. I couldn't handle it. God wanted everything, and I had given Him nothing of value. I had failed to live up to the requirement. Unlike Daniel, I had gone into captivity and eaten all the detestable foods. I had done everything I wasn't supposed to do, and I had no way of reversing any of it.

How do we really do the will of God? How do we do what Daniel did? Where does that kind of boldness come from, and how on earth do we get it? These are the questions I had as I began to sit in the presence of God. These are the questions that ran through my head. I had come to take hold of the feet of Jesus, knowing that He paid the price for me. I knew that my sins had been forgiven, and I knew that He had made me new. Now, I struggled to see how I would keep heading toward Him and not turn back to my old life. I had found a Savior, and I felt this urge to do the work and will of God. My problem was that every time I had ever attempted to step out and speak God's Word or love someone like Christ loved us, my boldness quickly fled. Every time I had attempted to stand up to temptation, my frailties trampled over my hope. My weakness and rampant insecurities always won out against my desire to please God.

As I prayed about my weaknesses, I believe God revealed the key in the story of Daniel. Later in Daniel's life, he was called upon to interpret a dream for King Belshazzar. As Daniel stood before him, the king said:

"Now I have heard about you that a spirit of the gods is in you, and that illumination, insight and extraordinary wisdom have been found in you."

Daniel 5:14

The king recognized that it wasn't Daniel who was at work, but there was a greater power at work in him. Daniel could do what no other man in the kingdom could do because the Spirit of God was with him. Daniel could do the will of God because God was doing His will through him. If we would really step back and look at ourselves, we would realize that there isn't anything we can do on our own. Try to breathe without using the breath given to you by God. Try to see without using the eyes God gave you. You can't do it. In the same way, we cannot take a step forward in God's will without God Himself acting with us.

So if it's His Spirit that we need, we have to ask the question: How can fallen human beings be filled with God's Spirit? On our own, we are covered in sin and shame. No matter who you are, you have sinned and fallen short of the glory of God. How then can we sinners be filled with His Spirit? You might be thinking, *Well that's easy. It's what you've been saying this whole time. We need to seek Him to find Him, right? That is how we invite the Holy Spirit to fill us.* I'm glad you are still reading this book, because I'm about to flip everything on its head.

Earlier, I told you that I was going to discredit the argument against the existence of God that says a loving God would not allow bad things to happen to good people. Here's the reason that claim doesn't line up with God's actions throughout history: there are no good people. God is good—He is perfect, and anything apart from Him is not good. So, if we choose to sin just one time, we completely separate ourselves from His presence, and from His goodness. Because of the fall of man, every human being is born with a sinful, fleshly nature. No amount of good works we do can make up for our bad.

God does not let bad things happen to good people, because apart from Him, there are no good people. Adam and Eve sinned for the first time in the Garden of Eden, and since then every single human being has been born with the innate tendency toward sin. (Romans 5:12-21) You don't have to teach a child to do the wrong things. You have to teach a child to do what's right. Creation itself also suffered a curse when Adam and Eve sinned. Bad things happen to people, not because God is being negligent, but because we live in a world that is suffering the effects of the curse of sin. However, thankfully, God can still use negative circumstances to point us to our need for Him, and that does not change His goodness. Through His Spirit at work in us, we can even overcome the sin nature with which we were born.

There's one problem with our natural attempts to receive His Spirit though: as imperfect beings, we cannot have His Holy Spirit dwell in us, no matter how much we seek Him. It is impossible. God's Spirit is perfect and cannot dwell with imperfection. No amount of waiting on or seeking God will ever draw you close enough to Him to be filled with the Holy Spirit.

I know this seems at odds with what I said previously, but there's a foundational truth behind everything I said that you must understand in order to move forward. When I first started seeking God, I thought that my *effort* was leading me to Him. At the time, I could not see that it was actually my childlike *belief* in Him that led the way. I sought God because I *believed* that He would do what He had promised. Once I began to believe that God was speaking truth, my belief (faith) led me to take action.

Growing up, I had placed so much weight on my own efforts, that it was nearly impossible for me to see that salvation was not about my attempts to please God. I received salvation the moment when I finally understood that it was all about His work on the cross. All God expected of me was a childlike belief. When I believed in Jesus, trusting that His blood covered my sins, I received forgiveness, freedom, and righteousness.

A true gift is not something that is earned, and God gave us a perfect gift. God sent His perfect Son, Jesus Christ, to earth so that whoever believes in Him will have life. *So you are saying everything boils down to one simple thing?* Yes. The day you are set free is not the day you put enough effort into seeking God. The day you are set free is the day you believe. What Jesus says about belief in the gospels will astound you, and I encourage you to go read His words. When you read His words and believe them, your life is turned upside down. Better than that, when you read His words and believe them, you experience His life in you. It is *belief in Jesus* that allows us to receive the Holy Spirit. Jesus has said in Luke 11:13:

> *"If you then, being evil, know how to give good gifts to your children, how much more will your heavenly Father give the Holy Spirit to those who ask Him?"*

Jesus talks about asking God for the Holy Spirit, however, why would you ask if you did not first *believe* that Jesus was telling the truth? Even if you asked, just to see what would happen, you could not ask in faith apart from truly believing His words, and we know that anything not done in faith is sin (see Romans 14:23). Because of this, believing is a prerequisite to receiving the Spirit.

Some people get heated over whether or not you receive the Holy Spirit at the moment of salvation or if being filled with the Spirit is a separate occurrence. I'm not going to get into a theological debate over this issue, but I will speak from my own experience. My salvation was the start of a beautiful friendship with Jesus through the Spirit inside of me. However, there have also been times when I have been seeking Him that I have more fully experienced the effects of His presence. So, in short, I believe we do receive God's Spirit when we are saved, but I also believe we can ask for His Spirit to more fully fill our thoughts, actions, and lives. Just because you have a relationship with someone does not mean that relationship is all it could be. Similarly, I'm not going to stop seeking the Lord just because I've received salvation. I want His Spirit to be continuously free to do anything He desires to do in and through me.

Let me get back to my point. We receive salvation the same way we receive the Spirit: through faith. Our righteousness is a gift from God that only comes through belief in His Son. I believe that the most popular verse in the entire Bible has lost its power because we have misinterpreted its meaning. Jesus says in John 3:16:

"For God so loved the world, that He gave His only begotten Son, that whoever believes in Him shall not perish, but have eternal life."

Eternal life, freedom in Christ, and forgiveness from sins is found only through belief in Jesus. Belief in Jesus is the *only* way, and Jesus backs up this truth by calling Himself the *Way* (John 14:6). I've had a lot of people over the years say to me, *"I've done too much to be forgiven. I've made too many mistakes, and there's no way God could ever forgive me."* This was exactly the way I felt in college. I could see the severity of my own sin, and I could feel the weighty guilt that followed it. Sin's nature is the opposite of God's nature. God is good, and God is love, and sin apposes these things. It is self-seeking, arrogant, immoral, evil, and hateful, and my heart had been full of these characteristics. On top of this, sin is also a liar. It promises freedom and happiness, but it delivers oppression, shame, and misery. I have never been so depressed and miserable as I was when I was entrenched in sin, trying to satisfy my fleshly desires. The worst part about sin is that, when you're ruled by it, you are constantly drawn back to it—back to your shameful state. The truth is that none of us can escape it. Sin ultimately leads us to death— an eternity of separation from God. However, the good news is that, even though sin wants to take everything from us, Jesus gave everything He had for us. We see this truth in Romans 6:23:

"For the wages of sin is death, but the free gift of God is eternal life in Christ Jesus our Lord."

The gift of righteousness in Jesus is exactly that: a *gift*. When Jesus allowed Himself to be beaten, stripped, pierced, whipped, and crucified, He took your sin on Himself. Your sin and my sin were dumped on Him on the cross. He carried it all, and He died as payment for that sin. It makes sense that there should be punishment for all the sin that we have committed. I struggled greatly with this idea after first realizing that I was a sinner. I knew that my actions were evil, and I believe that I would have to pay for them. What I missed was the truth that Jesus also knew that someone would have to pay for our sins. Because of God's love for us, Jesus came down to earth, and He paid for our heavy sin with His own death.

Did you know that the word *gospel* literally means *good news?* The day that I believed what God had done on my behalf, it was good news to my soul. The debt had been paid, and my part was to believe in the finished work of Jesus on the cross.

Believe it or not, you can choose to believe. That may sound ridiculous, but it's true. You have a choice to make. The Bible doesn't say Abraham was given a greater faith that enabled him to believe God. Romans 4:3 simply says:

"Abraham believed God, and it was credited to him as righteousness."

Stop doubting and believe. Believe in what Jesus has done. When you do this, God credits you with the righteousness of His Son. In a sense, Jesus offered us a trade. He took our sin, and He offered us His righteousness. When we believe, God no longer sees the stains of sin on us. Instead, He sees the perfect image of His Son living in us.

So, I started with belief, and my actions soon followed. When you choose to truly believe, your desires change. Suddenly, you want to seek God because you want to be as close as possible to the One who has saved you. When you are living in belief, you desire to read His Word and follow it because you want to live out all the promises and truth that He has spoken. Knowing God's promises is important because they paint a picture of what we can expect from Him. When we are walking in belief, we are waiting for His promises to occur instead of wondering if they ever will. When we believe God, our lives undergo a transformation. Jesus begins to live through us to accomplish His good work. When this happens, our lives are no longer our own. Through His Spirit working in us, we can begin to love others the way He has loved us.

I was not set free because I spent time and effort seeking God. I was set free simply because one day I chose to believe what He said. Once I firmly decided that I was going to believe God, I responded to my belief by taking a step of faith. My ability to act in faith did not come from me, though. It came from God. Did you know that God has given each of us a measure of faith? (see Romans 12:3) It isn't up to us to determine how much faith we start out with, but it is up to us to choose to act on that faith. Romans 1:17 states:

"For in it the righteousness of God is revealed from faith to faith; as it is written, 'But the righteous man shall live by faith.'"

The reason the righteous shall live by faith is because they *have to* live by faith in order to be righteous. It's not as if all the righteous people are granted more faith then everyone else. The truth is, no one is righteous on their own. The Bible says, "There is no one who does good, not even one" (Psalm 14:3b). So what does it mean that the righteous will live by faith? It simply means, those who put their faith (belief) in Jesus are made righteous through His blood. So, to be righteous, you have to have faith, and you have to use it. To be righteous, you have to believe that God is telling the truth. The Bible says, "Abraham was justified by faith." That means that he was eternally rewarded for simply believing what God had said. Jesus even said in John 6:29:

"This is the work of God, that you believe in Him whom He has sent."

If you can't tell, I really want you to get this. I want you to get it because, if you miss faith in Jesus, you miss everything. Romans 10:8-10 plainly states this same truth. It says:

"But what does it say? 'The word is near you, in your mouth and in your heart'—that is, the word of faith which we are preaching, that if you confess with your mouth Jesus as Lord, and believe in your heart that God raised Him from the dead, you will be saved; for with

the heart a person believes, resulting in righteousness, and with the
mouth he confesses, resulting in salvation."

Receiving salvation does not mean being allowed into heaven despite your unrighteousness. Receiving salvation means being made righteous because your sins were washed away. The reason that Jesus is the only Way is because He is the only one who can wash our sins away. His blood is the only payment. This idea continues with verses 11 through 13 of the same chapter. It says:

"For the Scripture says, 'Whoever believes in Him will not be disappointed.' For there is no distinction between Jew and Greek; for the same Lord is Lord of all, abounding in riches for all who call on Him; for 'Whoever will call on the name of the Lord will be saved.'"

Once you get this, your life will never be the same. If God says I will never be disappointed when I believe in Him, then I've really got something to get excited about. Another translation says that we will "not be put to shame" (ESV). Not being put to shame means that none of my sins or failures or mistakes will weigh me down. None of my mishaps are going to get the best of me. Nothing can make me unclean because the blood of Christ has made me clean. Does that mean I can head right back into sin because I'm covered? Not at all. As I mentioned before, true belief leads you to act in faith. It transforms you by allowing Jesus to live in you and work through you. When that happens, you won't want to return to sin anymore. You'll wake up each day with a longing to draw closer to your Savior and to continue being changed by Him.

This verse from Romans also says that God richly blesses all who call on Him. You can be certain that if you believe God, He is going to treat you as if you have had no sin on you at all. If you believe God, He is going to treat you as a righteous son or daughter. The reason He will treat you as if you are righteous is because you will *be* righteous. When your sins are washed away, every part of you is cleansed. If you believe that Jesus is Lord—that He died for you and was raised again on the third day, God will give you *His* righteousness. This is not just good news; it is really good news. Romans 4:8 says it beautifully:

"Blessed is the man whose sin the Lord will not take into account."

This is the rich blessing from God I was talking about. The blessing we get to receive is the same blessing God made to Abraham. Abraham believed, so he was made righteous. If you believe, you will be made righteous—none of your sins will be counted against you! I know I'm camping out on this idea, but it's crucial. It's the foundation that every other aspect of the Christian walk is built on. My desire is that, if you aren't already, you will be filled with the Spirit by the end of this book. However, it's essential that you first understand the amazing gift of grace God has given us through His Son. Galatians 3:13-14 makes the connection between receiving salvation and receiving the Holy Spirit. Listen to these words:

"Christ redeemed us from the curse of the Law, having become a curse for us—for it is written, 'Cursed is everyone who hangs on a tree'—in order that in Christ Jesus the blessing of Abraham might come to the Gentiles, so that we would receive the promise of the Spirit through faith."

It says it all right there. By faith we can receive the righteousness that Abraham received. By faith, we can receive the promise of the Spirit.

Some of us have heard about righteousness by faith before—maybe we've heard it our whole lives. That doesn't mean we're incapable of believing a lie, though. A thought can arise that says, *You've still got to do something to get the Holy Spirit of God to dwell inside you. You've still got to make some effort. Walking with the Holy Spirit and hearing from God is a privilege reserved for ultra-spiritual believers.* If any doubt like this remains in your mind, listen to me. Galatians 3 makes it clear that we receive righteousness and the Spirit the same way. There is nothing you can do to receive salvation except believe. You receive God's Holy Spirit the same way—through belief. It is belief in the words of God that motivates you to take the specific steps of faith laid out in Scripture. When we confess Jesus with our mouths, we are responding to the belief in our hearts. When we ask to receive the Spirit, we are responding to belief.

Salvation and the Holy Spirit are promises of God. There isn't anything you can do to receive God's promises, except to believe. You might be thinking, *but I've got to do the work of God.* What did Jesus say was the work of God? The New Living Translation writes John 6:29 this way:

"Jesus told them, 'This is the only work God wants from you: Believe in the one he has sent.'"

Are we never supposed to do anything else? The truth is, yes. You are never supposed to do anything else, because you cannot do anything else. Remember, we cannot do anything on our own (John 15:5). God does expect you to do His will—to act in faith— however, you will never be able to do it on your own. Once you believe and are filled with His Spirit, it will no longer be you doing it. Instead, Jesus Christ will be working through you. True belief is followed by steps of faith, but those steps are not steps you could ever take on your own. In Galatians 2:20, Paul says:

"I have been crucified with Christ; and it is no longer I who live, but Christ lives in me; and the life which I now live in the flesh I live by faith in the Son of God, who loved me and gave Himself up for me."

The only thing you are required to do is to believe what God has said. The only thing you are required to do is to trust in Jesus Christ. Once His Spirit is in you, He will do the rest. Does that mean we can sit back and go limp? No. Paul gets specific about the ongoing requirement. He makes it clear that he lives by faith in the Son of God. Jesus in him is doing the work, but it's his job to continue doing the one thing God has asked of him—to continue believing. Some of us believed in Jesus to save us at one point, but we aren't living in belief. God's required work is to believe, and He has already given you a measure of faith. Even if you have the smallest amount of faith, you have enough faith to believe in Jesus. You might not have faith to move mountains right now, but you can believe, and that's all that God is asking for.

The Pharisees did everything they thought God had required of them, but they missed the one thing that mattered. I believe this verse from Romans was written because of people like them:

"And Isaiah is very bold and says, 'I was found by those who did not seek Me, I became manifest to those who did not ask for Me.'"

Romans 10:20

Some of the Jews missed Jesus when He was standing right in front of them, because they did not believe that He was who He said He was. Because of this, Isaiah prophesied about the Gentiles finding God. He was talking about those who would come to God and receive His favor by believing in His Son Jesus Christ. He was talking about you and me. You see, we are not capable of simply living a life that is pleasing to God. The Pharisees were not able to do it, and neither are we. The only thing we have been given the ability to do is to make a choice. That choice is simply this; to truly believe in Jesus or to not believe in Him.

The fact that God desires to work through us is good news, but I have potentially sad news as well. If you do not see the work of God being done in you, then you may need to question whether or not you have actually believed at all. If the Spirit of God lives inside of you, then the inside of you ought to be bubbling up with His Spirit. His life ought to be flowing out of you. A constant transformation should be occurring, and if this change is not happening, I want you to stop and seriously consider what you have believed. Remember, Jesus talked about those who would say, "Lord, Lord," and yet never knew Him. They believed that they were doing good works and making a difference, but they failed to believe *Him*. We can do everything right in our own eyes, but if we miss Jesus Christ, then we have done all of our work in vain. God bought you with a heavy price by sending His Son to die. That gift is laid out before you. You can choose to believe your new Master, or you can choose to go back to the old master.

God never said, "Go to church enough and you will be saved." God never said, "Try to love people and you will be saved." He didn't say, "Just follow your heart and you will be saved." Now, God did say, "Love your neighbor as yourself," but even this we cannot do unless Jesus Christ is doing it through us. Without Him, we cannot do it. We cannot uphold the law, and God knows this. That is exactly why he sent a payment that would take the punishment away from us. He sent His Son to carry the burden of sin and death so that we could be set free. Do you really want to be set free? Think about all that junk. Think about all that stuff that you have carried—all the shameful memories. Now think about Jesus on that cross. He did not hang there thinking, "Someday, one of My followers is going to remember Me hanging here and it will give them the courage to make up for their mistakes." No. Jesus hung there, beaten and bruised—knowing that someday, you would believe in Him and be completely set free.

If you are set free from sin by believing in Jesus, then why do you even need the Holy Spirit? I want to give you two reasons. First, the Holy Spirit assures you of your salvation. He confirms it to you, even when you face times of doubt. Before I was filled with the Spirit, I constantly wondered if I was really saved or not, even after devoting my life to Christ. The best way to know that you have received salvation is to hear God Himself, through the Holy Spirit, telling you that you are saved. When the doubt arises, He reminds you of the cross. When the shame tries to surface, He brings to memory the truth of His sacrifice. Second, the blood of Jesus sets you free from the punishment of sin, but the life of Christ, through the indwelling of the Holy Spirit, sets you free from the power of sin. Have you ever faced a sin that you feel like you can never overcome? Jesus promised the Holy Spirit to us so that we could have victory over the hold of sin in our lives.

I know the Holy Spirit is a sensitive subject to some, because I know that there has been a lot of misrepresentation out there—especially in the charismatic arena. If you're afraid of asking God to fill you with His Spirit because of spectacles you have seen on television or at specific churches, please understand something. You witnessed people being weird, but you may not have witnessed a real movement of the Holy Spirit. The Holy Spirit will not make you crazy, and He won't force Himself upon you. He is God, and God is good.

God is the Father, the Son, and the Holy Spirit—He is three in one. If you have rejected the work of the Holy Spirit in your life, then you have unfortunately rejected part of God's plan for your life. The strange activity in some churches that has been presented as a work of the Sprit has made it easy for the devil to foster a lie in the minds of believers. If he can get you to believe that the Holy Spirit is Someone you should stay away from, then he has blocked you from experiencing the fullness of God's plan for your life. If the Holy Spirit is a promise given to us directly from Jesus, then wouldn't the devil want to stop us from receiving that promise? If you've never experienced the working of the Holy Spirit in your life, I believe that God is speaking to your heart right now, and I believe He is saying it's time to ask.

- 9 -

Spiritual Boldness

Once I began to believe, everything changed. Everything changed because I knew that there was an all-powerful God living inside of me. God began to establish His boldness inside of me—a boldness that I had never known before. I began to feel His presence with me even during mundane activities. I had allowed fear to control my actions and words, but now courage arose within me, prompting me to speak the Word of God. When one of my friends would bring up a subject, my mind would immediately relate it with something I had read in God's Word the day before. I would interrupt conversations, saying things like, "That sounds just like what David in the Bible was going through," or "Here's what God has said about that struggle." What I had once thought to be cheesy was now relevant and powerful, because now I believed it. I began to apply Scripture to my life. When a problem arose, I spoke to it with the Word of God. I said, "I am more than a conqueror through Him who loves me," or "I can do all things through Christ who strengthens me," or "If God be for me, who can be against me?" The promise that God was for me had never really helped until the day I believed that He actually was.

As I began to seek the Lord on a regular basis, the Spirit of God continued to speak to me. He would interrupt me at times, telling me things I had never even asked to know. One time, I was in a camp worship service when the Holy Spirit suddenly spoke to my heart. He said, *I have something for you to say to that guy standing next to you.* I didn't even know the guy's name, but I knew that something powerful was happening inside me. I felt the presence of God, but more than that, I believed that God was with me. I leaned over to the guy and said, "Hey, what's your name?" He said, "Ethan." I said, "I feel like God has something for me to tell you and it's simply this: He hears you." That was all I believed God had told me to say, and I was unsure if it would mean anything to the young man or not.

Unexpectedly, the moment those words left my mouth, I lost my strength. I fell down into my chair, confident that God had just done something through me I could never have done on my own. Ethan put his hand on his heart, and he began to cry. Then he simply said, "Thank you." It was only a few weeks after that when one of my friends began to tell me about Ethan and the issues he was facing. He said that his mother was battling a severe illness, and I wondered if that was what he could have been praying about that night at camp.

During my lifetime, I've struggled with attempting to be truly humble. What I've learned is that to allow God to speak through you, you must allow yourself to come humbly before Him. There is no getting around it. When the Creator of the universe, in all His wisdom and knowledge, has decided to use you, there isn't any getting around being humble. When the voice of God speaks to you, all of your pride goes out the window. His presence shows who we are, and it reveals who He is. We are just dust, but God is God. We are made from dirt, yet God has loved us with a perfect, radical love. He desires to spend eternity with us, but He also desires for us to intimately know Him. In the midst of our filth and hopelessness, God's Son breaks through and fills us with hope. When we see God for who He really is and when we understand what He did for us, no amount of pride can remain. Some of us have an attitude that says, *I'm going to get what I want, and then I'll let you have the rest, God.* Yet, we wonder why we seldom experience the presence or power of God. Should we not rather say in our hearts, *God, I'm so very small. I am made from dirt, and yet You, an all-knowing, all-powerful God, have loved me so very much. Thank you! Your will be done, Lord—not mine.*

The crazy thing about learning this truth is that I often still approached God with a spirit of pride. I still do to this day, because no one is perfect, but it was a daily struggle when I first started out. One day during my senior year of college, I prepared to drive out of the gym parking lot after cheerleading practice. I had been praying and thinking about the Holy Spirit constantly throughout that semester, and many unanswered questions rested in my mind. I stopped the car at the edge of the parking lot and turned on my left blinker. Suddenly, I felt God tugging on my heart. In my spirit, I heard the phrase, *Go home the other direction.* I weighed the distance in my mind, and I decided that it would be a shorter trip if I took a left and still went home the way I had planned. Before I could press the gas pedal, I heard it again. *Go home the other direction.* In my mind, I perceived a picture of a stop sign at the end of a road. It was next to a baseball field. I recognized it, and I knew that if I turned right, I would have to stop at that stop sign on my way home.

However, I chose not to listen. I had already made up my mind to turn left, so I started home on my normal route. I had only driven about fifty feet, when I once again heard a voice in my spirit. *You want to know me? Turn around. There is something that will happen at that stop sign.* Again, the image of the stop sign at the end of the road next to the baseball park filled my mind. Finally, I gave in. I said, "Okay, I'm turning around. If You want to show me something, then let's go." I drove the other direction for a while and soon ended up at the stop sign that I had clearly seen. I halted my vehicle and sat there for a few seconds. Peering around, I could see nothing out of the ordinary. In fact, I didn't see anyone in any direction.

Waiting for only a few moments, I quickly decided to drive on. I tried to ignore the words I had heard for the minutes that followed, but eventually a thought came to my mind, "See, there wasn't anything there." And that was that. I had listened to God's pull on my heart, and I had shown God that it didn't pay off. If He was trying to convince me of something, it hadn't worked. I figured I must have simply been hearing my own thoughts, wishing that I could hear from God. Looking back, it's funny how God let me reason through disappointment before He showed me what He wanted to show me. I arrived at my apartment five minutes later. As I stepped into the front door, my phone rang. The name of a good friend of mine, who was also a former roommate, appeared on my phone.

"Hey, man! What's up?" I said, assuming the call to be random.

"Troy, dude. I was just calling because I saw you in your car about five minutes ago."

"You did?" I asked, "Where?"

"You were parked at a stop sign."

"Which stop sign?"

"One of the ones close to the school."

"No, which stop sign?"

"The one at the end of the road next to the baseball field. Anyway, I saw you parked there and I realized we haven't talked in a while. What are you doing for dinner? Want to come over?"

I was shocked. I wanted to go back and undo what I had said in my mind just minutes before. At that moment, I was unsure why God had wanted my friend to call me, but it was obvious that He had a reason. I did go over for dinner that night, and at one point, the subject of the Holy Spirit came up. After eating, we had an in-depth, two-hour-long conversation about the Holy Spirit and His involvement in the life of the believer. As I sat and talked with my friend, several of my questions were answered. I remember wondering why I had never heard my friend talk about the Holy Spirit before, but it didn't matter. God was using him to teach me. After leaving that night, I had to admit to myself that God was always going to be right.

If we can get to that point, where we believe that God actually knows what He's doing, it will be much easier for us to step out in faith when we need to. I have sometimes had the thought, *God, I'll step out in faith again and listen to You, but if You don't come through this time then that's it. Don't expect me to keep doing this.* The truth is that God will come through every time. He will always back up His word. If God has actually said He would do something, then He is going to do it, no matter how impossible it may seem to us. When we hear from Him, but make the decision to keep heading in our own direction, things stay the same. When we step back and say, "God, take me wherever You want me to go," things begin to change. If you give God the reins of your life—if you let Jesus be your Master, a lot is going to change.

I know it sounds ideal to those who have believed to live in total submission to God, but what normally ends up happening? We don't want to give things over to Him because that would mean giving up our own plans. So, we pretend. We make believe. We go around making sure that we do everything we can to look like we are living for God, and yet we mask the real intentions of our hearts. We attend church, we say nice things, we give something, and we go to a Bible study or sing praise songs. Yet, this is not what God ultimately wants from us. He would rather have our willingness to be led by Him.

Some of us are doing these things, thinking we are getting away with serving God while living for ourselves, and yet we don't realize that God is not impressed. God doesn't just want what we can give Him on a Sunday. God wants us. He wants our whole hearts.

Isaiah 29:13-15 speaks about people that did something similar. Before you read these verses, I want you to know something. I'm not including verses like this to heap guilt on you, because then I would also heap guilt upon myself. I'm not perfect, and I know you aren't either. God does not expect us to be perfect in our performance. However, He does desire us to hold onto the work of Christ with our whole beings, trusting fully in His grace and love. That takes submissiveness, and it takes humility. As we do that, He changes our hearts so that we can better walk with Him, following His leading. The reason I include verses like this is because I want you to know God. My goal is that you will come away from this book with a deeper, more intimate relationship with Jesus Christ. With that in mind, let's see what Isaiah says:

"Then the Lord said, 'Because this people draw near with their words and honor Me with their lip service, but they remove their hearts far from Me, and their reverence for Me consists of tradition learned by rote, therefore behold, I will once again deal marvelously with this people, wondrously marvelous; and the wisdom of their wise men will perish, and the discernment of their discerning men will be concealed.'

Woe to those who deeply hide their plans from the Lord, and whose deeds are done in a dark place, and they say, 'Who sees us?' or 'Who knows us?'"

I could have continued to drive home my usual way, thinking that I was right and God was wrong. Because I turned the car around, God did something that blew me away. Even when I puffed up with pride and thought, *God, I would be right in going my own way,* God still had His plan in mind, and He was still going to do something mighty in my life. He didn't give up on reaching me simply because my car was headed in the wrong direction. The downside about me doubting Him for a moment was that I ended up looking a little foolish. I stopped listening as soon as God appeared to have made a mistake, and yet God was still gracious. The big problem is that we often don't listen in the first place. We often don't want to hear what God has to say because we want a left turn in life and we don't want anyone to stop us. We have an agenda in mind, and allowing God to show us another way would ruin our plans. However, God wants to show us, not just *another* way, but a *better* way. His plans are so much greater than our own. Isaiah 55:6-7 reveals this:

> *"Seek the Lord while He may be found; call upon Him while He is near. Let the wicked forsake his way and the unrighteous man his thoughts; and let him return to the Lord, and He will have compassion on him, and to our God, for He will abundantly pardon."*

God has compassion on us when we admit that we need Him—when we admit that His way is better. In verse 8, God says, "For My thoughts are not your thoughts, nor are your ways My ways," and in verse 9 He says, "For as the heavens are higher than the earth, so are My ways higher than your ways and My thoughts than your thoughts." I saw myself as a fool when I realized that God's way had been the right way. I wanted to go back and try again and believe Him fully from the start, but all I could do was to say, "I was wrong, and You were right. Your ways are better than my ways." As I said this, He reminded me of His amazing grace.

Allowing the Lord to lead you is not meant to be a fear-filled process. He's our Father, our Friend, and our Savior. God knows that we are not going to get it right every time, and He has made provision for our learning curve. He is the one who abundantly pardons, even when we choose to disobey. You might be thinking, *My problem is not disobedience; I'm just not sure how to hear from God.* Here are some practical steps: be humble, seek Him, ask for the Holy Spirit, obey, and read the Word. These actions all follow belief. When we believe what God has said about Jesus in His Word, He is going to live in us and we are naturally going to want to do these things.

When we humble ourselves before God, trusting Him to lead us down straight paths—paths that are better than our own—He will begin to make those paths clear. Seeking Him is simply part of our relationship with Christ; we pursue Him because we want to be closer to Him. To be filled with the Holy Spirit, Jesus told us that we simply need to ask. Once we do hear from God, either through the Bible or the Holy Spirit, we need to be obedient if He has asked us to do something. However, it's critical to always compare God's voice to the written Word of God. If you think the Holy Spirit is telling you something that doesn't line up with Scripture, then you can trash it because that's not from Him. God is never going to disagree with His Word. He remains the same, and His Word will never fail.

I am thankful I decided to step out in faith and finally turn right that day, because I got to see the plan of God being fulfilled in my life. Oftentimes, we aren't even willing to take the first step. We want to seek God with our mouths only because we don't want Him spoiling our plans. When I made God the navigator of my life, it did spoil my plans. Everything I had ever wanted was flushed down the tubes. All my own dreams and aspirations were replaced. Everything I had been working toward was lost, and it has been the greatest loss I have ever experienced. You see, when God takes over, He replaces your desires. He alters your compass, adjusting the course of your life. What is crazy is that, no matter how hard we try to hide our plans from God, we never really can. God always knows our hearts. It's a good thing that when we turn from our own ways and say, "God, help me," He is gracious and pardons our every sin. When we look to Him, He makes us whole. He points us in the right direction. He fills us with His presence and gives us hope for tomorrow.

This is what it means to no longer live so that Christ can live through you (Galatians 2:20). When Jesus is at the forefront of your thoughts, you are continuously moving in the direction God wants you to go. I'm thankful it's not up to us because on our own, we could never keep moving in the right direction. Only His Spirit and His grace give us the strength to live for Him. If you aren't filled with His Holy Spirit, don't wait another second. Please don't wait. God has a great plan for you that He desperately desires to see you fulfill. He has a purpose for you that you cannot even begin to imagine. He has something for you to do, people for you to reach, and a hope for you to hold onto that will never run out. Don't stop seeking Him until you are caught up in His grace and His abundant love. Don't look to the right or the left. Just keep your eyes focused on Jesus.

When Peter stepped out of the boat, he didn't say, "Well Jesus I'm going to head that other direction over there for a bit, and then I'll come back to you." No. He knew that his best chance of walking on water was to be pointed directly at Jesus. He understood that the only way he was going to survive the storm was to be heading toward Jesus. Why do we sometimes jump out of the boat thinking we can head in our own direction? You aren't walking on your own. It's only by His grace and His work in your life. Look at Him. It's amazing what God does when you simply take the time to look at Him.

What storms are you talking about? If you had this thought, then just wait and see. When I first found Jesus, I thought everything was going to be a breeze from then on. Little did I know that a hurricane was on its way, and I was going to have to hold onto Jesus just to stay alive. Let's talk about that a little later. For now, I want to talk about wrestling.

- *10* -

Junior Year

When I said let's talk about wrestling, I didn't mean the sport. Sorry for those of you who enjoy a good wrestling bout. I was referring to what Paul talked about in Ephesians chapter 6, verse 12:

"For our struggle is not against flesh and blood, but against the rulers, against the powers, against the world forces of this darkness, against the spiritual forces of wickedness in the heavenly places."

I grew up hearing the King James Version of this verse, which uses the term *wrestle* instead of *struggle*. Either way you phrase it, that was exactly what became evident to me after I started to seek God. Though I had failed to realize it, spiritual forces had been at work against me the whole time I had been lost in sin too. I remember waking up on multiple occasions and having hallucinations, hearing things that were not there. After waking up from a nap one afternoon, I even sat up in bed, fully awake, but unable to control myself. I could see my roommate sitting across the room, turned away from me. I tried to yell his name, but I could not open my mouth. Fear had gripped me, and all I could think to do was call out for Jesus in my mind. This all happened before that night when I decided to put my trust in the Lord. Thankfully, because of the blood of the Lamb, I've never experienced anything like that since becoming a believer.

If you haven't noticed yet, we are in a spiritual war. I'm talking about angels and demons—the spiritual realm in which spiritual forces operate. If you don't believe in demons, yet you believe God's Word is true, I encourage you to read the gospels again. Jesus interacted with the spiritual world all the time, and one famous instance is found in Matthew 8:28-34. You might say, *I believe in angels and demons, but I don't believe they have any effect on our lives.* Before hearing from God, I thought the same thing. Take a look at Ephesians 6 again. The verse directly before what we read about struggling with spiritual forces makes it plain. Listen to what Paul says in verse 11:

"Put on the full armor of God, so that you will be able to stand firm against the schemes of the devil."

Other translations use the words *tactics* or *strategies* of the devil. If the Word of God is telling us we need to stand firm against the schemes, tactics, or strategies of the devil, then we can be sure that the devil is actually scheming against us. *But if the devil and demons are real, then how can we combat them? What on earth can we do against them?* The answer to this question is simple: nothing. We can do nothing against them when we operate in our own power. When a greater power (the power of Jesus Christ) is at work within you, you can do all things.

Growing up, I often encountered one of my deepest and darkest fears during a time when I had no control over the situation other than waking up. Some of the scariest things I faced as a child, and even as a teenager, were nightmares. When you dream, your mind explores new horizons, solves problems, and faces ideas it would not normally face.

I believe that God created our minds to dream for many reasons, but I also believe that God created our minds to dream peacefully. If we are not dreaming peacefully, something else has interrupted God's purpose behind our ability to dream. Some people attribute nightmares to eating the wrong thing or to dealing with stress, but I do not think that is always the case. Jesus tells us in John 10:10 that the devil's desire is to steal, kill, and destroy.

One of the fruits of the Spirit, provided by God Himself, is peace. If the devil is trying to steal from us, don't you think he's trying to steal the very things God provides? That's why he doesn't want us to sleep peacefully. You may be thinking, *That sounds scary.* If this is the case, then keep reading. We may face a scary enemy, but any spiritual force that has the guts to come up against our God is facing an even scarier one.

As a child, I understood that spiritual warfare was real. It wasn't until later that I began to doubt the enemy's influence in my life. It was obvious to my young self that, if I was having nightmares, Satan had something to do with it. There was no way any of that was coming from God. Sadly though, I had no way of protecting myself against attacks of the enemy while I was asleep. I eventually accepted the idea that I would have to live with the occasional nightmare. I had believed the lie that Satan was able to do what he liked while I was unconscious. After I would wake up, I would turn the lights on and read the Bible. I felt comforted while reading verses that reminded me of God's protection, but I seldom experienced the assurance that I needed. I would go back to sleep, resting on a shaky hope that the nightmares would cease. I was still afraid, and I did not break the cycle of fear until the day I discovered the real presence of Jesus Christ.

When I was filled with the Spirit of God during college, the presence about me changed. As I spent time seeking God, His presence covered me. Even better than that, when I simply *asked* for His presence, His presence covered me. Even as a young adult in college, I still had the occasional nightmare. What normally accompanied a nightmare was the awareness of a presence other than my own. It could be a ghost, a skeleton, or just a person who had a bad aura about them. In my dreams, I would be aware that something was wrong long before I ever encountered one of these beings. Whatever form it took, the spirit of fear was behind it. Most of my nightmares ended with me running. I often had no control over myself during dreams, so I would find myself running and trying to hide. Eventually, I would wake up sweating and terrified. One night, everything changed. I went to bed in the presence of Jesus—filled with His Spirit.

I was sleeping in my dorm room, dreaming peacefully, when suddenly my dream transitioned into a nightmare. In the dream, I was standing in a house with some other people. The house began to grow dark as everyone left. Then, as I walked through the hall into another room, I began to feel the same presence of fear that I always felt during a nightmare. I rounded the corner and saw a person standing in the middle of the room. The person was emanating fear. It was a normal nightmare all over again, except that something was different this time. Something had changed. I would have normally run, but this time, I stood my ground. In the past, I would have attempted to look away or hide, but now I stared him down. I stood my ground because I felt a third presence that I had never felt in a dream before. It was Jesus. I could feel His presence with me.

The spirit of fear was emanating from this figure in the room, but the Spirit of Jesus Christ was flowing from inside me. Then, everything changed. What had been an evil expression on the person's face had now transformed into an expression of disbelief. I was not afraid of him; He was afraid of me. I didn't even think about waking myself up. The person in the dream turned and began to run. He moved out of that room and into the next, so I chased him. He ran from room to room, trying to escape the presence that was inside of me, but he could not. Finally, he crouched down on the floor and covered his face with his hands.

I woke up from the dream full of energy, shaking my fist in the air. "That's right! Who's running now?" The presence of fear will always be overcome by the presence of Jesus Christ. Jesus can overpower anything that Satan tries to bring up against you. Reading enough verses of Scripture and singing enough songs in church never allowed me to walk in authority. I was given authority when I began to abide in the presence of Jesus Christ.

"What then shall we say to these things? If God is for us, who is against us?"

Romans 8:31

When God is with you, nothing can stand against you—nothing. When you walk in the presence of Jesus, you walk in peace and protection. I have had many dreams since where a strange presence has shown up, but none of them have been nightmares because I have the presence of Jesus Christ. They always run from me now because Jesus fights my battles with me. I'm no longer running; I'm standing on the Rock. King David knew that God's presence was the reason for his confidence. He wrote in Psalm 27:1:

"The Lord is my light and my salvation; Whom shall I fear?
The Lord is the defense of my life; Whom shall I dread?"

If you walk in the presence of Jesus Christ, you have no one to fear. If you walk in the presence of Jesus Christ, any power that comes up against you will be no match for the power within you. Here is the best part of this story: if they are running from me in my dreams, then they are doing the same thing while I'm awake. Spiritual warfare is not simply something that happens when we're asleep. One of the enemy's greatest tools is that subtle lie he whispers to us when we're wide awake. If he can get us to believe something contrary to God's Word then he has the opportunity to steal from us. However, you don't have to let the devil steal from you. He doesn't get to have dominion over your thoughts or emotions because you have the victory in Christ. Living in spiritual victory has nothing to do with your efforts. It's all because of Him who is with you. You can have victory because the authority of Jesus overcomes the powers of darkness.

You don't believe me when I say that we wrestle not against flesh and blood? Let me tell you another story. One time I was in my apartment, praying and reading God's Word. Though I had been praying for a while, I doubted whether or not God actually was there. I continued to pray, yet I continued to doubt. Finally, I thought, *I've had enough.* It was time to step out in faith, so I began to combat the enemy, the father of doubting.

I stood up, stretched out my hand, and said, "Satan, you take your spirit of doubt, and you leave right now in the name of Jesus Christ. I will not doubt any longer. I choose to believe. You take your spirit of fear, your spirit of doubt, and your spirit of unbelief and you get out of here. I am not afraid of you, and I will not allow you to continue to hinder me any longer." Then I took it a step further. I said, "God has said that without faith it is impossible to please God, so I will speak to you in faith. God is going to do amazing things in my life. He is going to use me to do great things, and there isn't anything you can do about it." I was taunting the devil, and I knew it. I was taunting him because I knew that God was with me, and if God was with me then no one could be against me—not even Satan himself.

You might be thinking, *Way to go!* Or you might be thinking, *You're crazy.* Either way, Satan didn't like what I said. I know this because of what happened next. I turned around and went straight to my room with the intention of going to bed. I lifted the covers back from my pillow, and there, underneath the sheets, I saw a sight that gave me goose bumps. All over my pillow and spread out under my covers and sheets were hundreds of ants. They had filled my bed and were swarming around in circles. The worst part was that they were in the shape of a human figure on my bed. I looked down at them in disbelief, feeling like I had just stepped into a scene from a horror film. Then I realized, I had bugged the devil, so the devil decided to bug me. I could only guess that he was furious at what I had said, and he wanted to get even. The funny thing is that when God is with you, nothing is ever even. God is always the victor, and He is always on top. So I laughed about the ants, shook my sheets off outside, threw them in the wash, and proceeded to sleep on the couch.

If you are thinking, *Are you saying that the devil has power to affect our lives?* I would answer by saying *Yes.* The devil has power because he was originally created with some power, however, all his power came from God. It still comes from God. Whatever happens to you or me, God knows about it beforehand. If you read the story of Job in the Bible, you will see that Satan had no authority to do anything to Job until God allowed him to do it. If it is Christ who lives in you, then whatever trials or tribulations come, God has signed off on them before they ever happen. If you are walking in

His will, then He has given them the okay because He knows He can use them for a greater purpose in your life.

If you are a believer, the devil has no authority to possess or control you. Light and darkness cannot dwell in the same place, and if you are a believer, you have the Light of the world living inside you. Though demons cannot possess you, you still can be influenced by the powers of darkness. Paul makes this clear when talking about anger in Ephesians 4. He warns us not to let the devil have an opportunity. He would not have warned believers not to give the devil an opportunity if they had no ability to open the door to the devil in the first place.

I'm scared to do anything because the devil might get me. Do you know how big God is? Do you know how great He is? Do you understand how awesome He is? If God, who far surpasses everything else in existence, is with you, then you have nothing to fear. Just knowing that God is big won't make you fearless though. You have to actually know *Him.* Jesus said in Luke 10:19:

"Behold, I have given you authority to tread on serpents and scorpions, and over all the power of the enemy, and nothing will injure you."

Who is Jesus talking to? Believers. He's letting His followers know that they have authority—His authority—on their side. Once you know Him, there isn't a thing that can stand up against you. Once He is working inside you, you've got nothing to worry about.

One time after college, I attended the church I had attended for most of my life growing up. One of my former pastors was speaking that night, and he told the story of Jesus and His disciples in the boat during the storm. The way in which he told the story stuck with me. This is a paraphrase, but he said something like this:

> While Jesus was sleeping in the boat, the disciples were freaking out over the storm. They were going crazy, thinking that they were all going to die. Imagine yourself as one of the disciples. What if, as a disciple in the boat, your greatest fear came true? What if the story ended there? The God of the universe sent his Son Jesus to the earth to die for our sins, but unfortunately He got stuck on a boat in a terrible storm. What if, unexpectedly, the boat sank and Jesus and all His disciples drowned that day. Oops. God didn't see that one coming! No. That's crazy.
>
> We laugh at the idea of Jesus drowning in the boat because we know that God is bigger and more sovereign than that. Now, I want you to apply this to your life. If you are a disciple of Jesus, then no matter how big the storms may seem; He is with you. If you are a disciple of Jesus, then no matter how huge those storms may look, just remember this: Jesus is in your boat.
>
> The idea of Jesus sinking and drowning with His disciples is silly because we know that would never happen. God obviously had a bigger plan in mind for Jesus, and He would never let something like a boat and a storm stop His mission from being fulfilled. As you come up against situations, even spiritual strongholds, that seem impossible for you to handle, remember who lives inside of you. If Jesus lives inside of you, then the devil is not simply coming against you, he is coming against Jesus Christ. Here's more good news: Jesus has already defeated him. If the devil is attacking you, it's only because he is trying to sidetrack you from accomplishing the plan that God has in mind for your life. If Jesus is with you, and you are abiding in Him, then you are going to see that plan come to completion. Romans 8:31 states this better than I ever could:

> *"What then shall we say to these things? If God is for us, who is against us?"*

- *11* -

After College

As I walked the stage to accept my degree, an undeniable inclination rose up inside of me: I believed I was headed for something great. I told myself that God had something tremendous in store for me, so I had every reason to be excited about my future. However, God's ideas for our lives do not always line up with our own. I temporarily moved back home with my parents, hoping to find a good job in the cinema industry.

At first, I only sent in a few applications, filled with certainty that offers would begin to flood in. As time passed, I admitted that it was going to be more difficult to find a job than I had initially thought. I started filling out countless applications online. I constricted my search to opportunities that had to do with my field of study, and I began to pray that God would provide me with a great job. As I prayed, I knew that God's Spirit was speaking to me, saying, *I have a great job in store for you.* I took Him at His word and kept applying.

As the days, weeks, and months went on, something inside me began to change. The thought began to arise that perhaps God had forgotten about finding me a job. Any time this thought would arise, I would set everything aside and seek Him. I would close my bedroom door, lie on the floor, and pray. I would say, "God, I know that you are my provider. You provide my every need according to Your riches in glory. I've got nothing to worry about because you are in control of this situation." Every time I would do this, I could feel the Holy Spirit working inside of me, helping my heart to trust Him, telling me that He had everything under control. Every time He said *Trust Me*, I believed Him. So, I kept applying. I kept applying because I continued to believe He had something great in store for me.

At first, I only applied for jobs in the field of cinematography or video production. I also had developed a good amount of knowledge regarding website development, and the thought occurred to me that perhaps I should broaden my scope. I had to pray about it, though, because I deeply desired to work in the world of cinema. For a while, I was hesitant to apply for web development positions, but I found peace about it when God said, *Apply*.

With that word, I began to apply to every job that I knew I the ability to do. Finally, I began to receive phone calls. I landed interviews with a few different companies. None of them, however, seemed to be right. One day, I went in for an interview with a Christian university, and they offered me a job that looked like the perfect fit. I would be working on exciting projects, it was a job related to my field of study, and the location would allow me to save money on rent because I could still live at my parents' house (which I was okay with doing). By the time this job offer appeared, I had gotten to the point where I was crying out to God every day saying, "God, please hear me! I need a job and I believe you have promised to provide one." I believed that those prayers were finally being answered. In every way, the opportunity felt perfect. The funny thing about perfection though, is that God is the only one who truly knows it when He sees it.

I thought the job was the solution to my problem, but God knew better. They asked me to accept, and they promised me a huge opportunity for my future. Before I could accept, though, I decided to go before God and give Him the job. I said, "God, if this is the job you want me to have, then I'll take it. If it's not, then I'll pass it by." I naturally assumed that God would say, *This is the job you've been waiting for. Take it.* I don't have to tell you how frustrated I felt when God said, *Don't take it.* I had come before Him in prayer, asking Him for His blessing, and He said *no*. I wanted to be certain about His answer, so I waited for a day, continuing to pray. However, I had no peace about accepting the job, and I knew that He was still saying, *No.*

Accepting a *no* from God can be a trying thing to do. If you're in the same boat that I was in, and God is answering your prayers in a way that you did not expect, it may help to look at it from another perspective. If you ever feel like you can't accept a negative answer from God, remember this: God's *no* is a *yes* for your future. God says no because He knows what is ultimately best for you.

God knows what you need, even when you think you know better than He does. As I searched for jobs, I assumed that my desires would be close enough to God's will to receive His blessing. However, God was revealing to me the importance of seeking His will first. Jesus emphasized this truth when He spoke to His brothers in John 7:6. It says:

"So Jesus said to them, 'My time is not yet here, but your time is always opportune.'"

He spoke about their desire for Him to travel with them to the festival. Whether they were sincere or not, they told Him that He should show himself before the people if He really wished to be famous. Jesus didn't listen to them. He did not allow Himself to listen to them because He prioritized the opinion of His Father. Any time for us is right, but that doesn't mean that it's the best time. I often come before God, saying, *God I need this right now,* or *God it's about time that I had this.* For a moment, this is the way I approached that job offer. I said, *God, I need this job* and God said, *No, you don't. I will provide.* That was that—I didn't argue any further. I called the university and told them that, after praying about the opportunity, I believed I was supposed to decline the offer. They told me that if I changed my mind I should call them back. I knew that I wouldn't.

I was beginning to believe to a greater extent that God really means what He says. When God says that He has something better in store for you than you could ever imagine, He is serious. As I hung up that phone, I felt full of faith. However, only three days later, I already regretted turning the job down. It didn't take long for me to let my faith be shaken. I started to doubt God's leading, and I wondered if I should call them back and ask if they would still take me on. If you ever find yourself facing a moment of doubt, you are not alone. It's in those weak moments when we are wrestling with our faith that we can often see God's hand clearly.

As Christians, we are going to face moments of weakness— when we feel like we don't have enough faith to do what God is asking us to do. The secret to following God's leading in those moments is to take your weakness directly to Him and lay it down at His feet. Tell Him about it. Be honest with God. Remember, His power is made perfect in our weakness (2 Corinthians 12:9). Inside my spirit, I knew that calling the university and taking that job was the wrong thing to do. So, I lay my fears down in prayer, trusting fully in His provision.

If you are seeking God, sometimes He is going to tell you to do things you don't understand. That is exactly what He did to me. At a point when I thought He was going to bring something great my way, He instead told me to do something that I thought was crazy. About a week after I turned down that job, one of my friends was over at my house. I overheard him telling my mom that he was going to be moving into an apartment by himself at The University of Texas at Arlington. Immediately, the weird idea of rooming with him came to my mind. I took it before the Lord and He said, *Move to Arlington*. As I prayed about it, it became clear that God had placed the idea into my mind.

Now, moving away from my parents' house seemed to me like a really dumb thing to do, especially since I only had enough money in my bank account to cover one month's rent. Even though it seemed stupid to me, God said, *Go*. So, I went. I moved in with my friend.

My parents drove the two and a half hours and helped me move all my stuff into my shared room. As I moved in, I didn't know what was going to happen. I didn't know where I would work, and I didn't know what God had in store. What I did know was that God had good plans. I *believed* that God had something great in store, even if it wasn't exactly what I had wanted. I continued to stand on the belief that God was telling the truth. Because I chose to react to the Holy Spirit in faith that week, now I get the joy of telling people what God did. As I stepped out in faith and obeyed the "dumb" thing He was telling me to do, He moved in my life. I went in for a random interview the next day, not fully realizing at first what sort of position I was applying for, and I got the job. As I listened to the job description and details, I realized the opportunity was entirely better than the job I had turned down.

You may be thinking, *Great. God did something awesome in your life. That doesn't mean He's going to do something awesome for me.* If you'll follow me for just a minute, I want you to think about the God you are talking about. Consider the expanse of His power— that He could create the known universe by simply speaking the words. Now, think about how much the same, awe-inspiring Creator of the universe has done for you, personally. He sent His only begotten Son to die—for you. God sent His Son to come down here, be tortured, be stripped of all dignity and honor, and then die for the sins of undeserving people like me and you. If God was willing to send Jesus to die, don't you think He is a God who wants to act on your behalf in the day-to-day? Romans 8:32 says it like this:

"He who did not spare His own Son, but delivered Him over for us all, how will He not also with Him freely give us all things?"

God is a gracious God. He is not like us—He isn't. Since God loves us so much that He would send His Son, Jesus, to die, I believe He loves us enough to provide for our every need as well. With that being said, please keep in mind the fact that the provision and promises of God do come with conditions. For example, we only receive the amazing grace of God when we choose to, in a state of repentance, believe in Jesus as our Lord and Savior. Jesus even talks about the supernatural provision of God following our decision to seek first His kingdom.

What should you do if you feel like your decisions have prevented you from receiving God's promises? Thankfully, it's in that moment when we accept just how undeserving we are that God desires to further reveal His love to us. Have you grasped the extent of His love for you? He loves us so much that our brains cannot even fully fathom it. There are times when I presume that I understand the measure of His love, but I know that I cannot. As long as we are on this earth, we will never completely understand the depth and height of His love. Ephesians 3:19 even tells us that the love of Christ "surpasses knowledge." That means that we can experience His love today, but if we are growing in our relationship with Him, we will always be experiencing it to a greater extent.

Because of God's love for us, we can trust that He has good plans in mind. Once we get to the point where we are trusting Him, and allowing His Word to change our hearts, then we'll start to see His good plans unfolding. Proverbs 3:5-6 says:

"Trust in the Lord with all your heart and do not lean on your own understanding. In all your ways acknowledge Him, and He will make your paths straight."

When I let go of the job that God asked me to pass up, I was choosing not to lean on my own understanding. I was choosing to trust in the Lord, placing my future completely in His hands. As I allowed Him to lead my decisions, I began to witness His provision at work. If you haven't realized it yet, God has a plan for you, and it's a *good* plan. God has something in mind for you that greatly exceeds anything that you could have in mind for yourself. If you will trust Him and listen to His call on your life, then He will cause His peace to fill you. He will cause His Spirit to lead you, and He will cause His love to overwhelm you. He has a plan, but it's up to you to lay down your plans long enough for Him to take over. God is good, and He loves you. You *can* believe it.

I began working for a well-known Christian broadcast ministry in September of 2011. I found myself in a challenging yet exciting position. I had been given a website development job, and I was getting to do some video work as well. At first, every project that I worked on seemed to complete itself. I was accomplishing tasks, and I believed that God was doing great things through me. I didn't know where God was taking me, but it was okay because I knew it was somewhere good. I knew it had to be—I believed it. It wasn't the fact that I was working for a Christian organization that I thought God was leading me. I understood that it was not my efforts that would allow God to work through me. Instead, it was still God's grace and power that would accomplish the work. It was His Spirit that was going to lead me where I needed to go—to do what I needed to do.

You might be thinking, *It sounds like you should have had no trouble then.* At first, this same thought ran through my head. If God was leading me and I was doing what seemed to be God's work for me—and on top of that I understood that God's grace and mercy enabled me to work—then I should have had no problems. As I started that new job, I had no idea how drastically my thinking would soon change.

A few months into my new job, my health levels began to shift. Slowly, my energy decreased. I kept ignoring it, writing it off as just a long-standing cold or lack of sleep, but I was about to find out that I was not just going to be able to shake it off. With every passing week, I grew more and more exhausted. The tiredness started showing up in the evenings after work, and then, it slowly spread so that it would come on sooner and sooner in the day. At the same time, an increasing weight of anxiety built up in my heart and mind. Even the slightest amount of anxiety would throw my body into a state of overwhelming fatigue.

Finally, during a weekend during which I visited my parents and siblings, my mom pointed out the fact that I looked terrible. She had noticed the dark circles around my eyes and the heaviness that encompassed my manner. I had already planned to take some time off a few weeks after that, so I figured I would wait until then to attempt a recovery. However, as I returned to work that week,

I felt as if I had lost my ability to function. I could not focus for more than a few minutes at a time, and I grew more and more tired with every second. Every weekday evening, I would head back to my apartment and attempt to sleep for as long as possible. Some nights I could sleep, but most nights were filled with small gaps of sleep amidst the long drawn out hours of lying on my bed wondering why I was still awake. I was facing a case of severe chronic fatigue while simultaneously battling an unexplainable insomnia. You can imagine what a bad combination that would be.

On top of all of this, I was completely alone. A few months into the job, I realized that the rooming situation would no longer work out, and I had moved to my own place. Now, I had no one. Besides the people I worked with, I knew no one. During the time between 5 p.m. and 8 a.m., I was left to face painful reality. The sickness had kept me in my apartment most of the time, and I had barely had a chance to try to make any friends in the new city. So anytime I wasn't working, the anxiety that follows extended isolation would attack. On a day that the fatigue would increase, I would attempt to sleep it off—barely finding any rest. Then, when some relief from the horrors of the illness would finally come, I would use the little time I had left to try to find someone to hang out with, and I would quickly realize again just how alone I was. I faced a seemingly endless circle of restlessness, and the tension in my body continued to build.

The feeling of loneliness ate at me. It tore me up on the inside. No matter how hard I tried to meet someone, or invite someone to hang out, everyone seemed to evade me. So, I stayed alone. I sat in my apartment for weeks and months, crying out to God. I cried and I cried. I yelled. I shouted. I pounded my fists against the floor over and over. As this cycle of deterioration steadily grew, my enthusiasm about God's plan faded, and I eventually reached the point where I felt like I had no hope left at all. I had come to the very end of my rope.

During the week, I would get up and go to work, hoping that someone at my job would ask about my situation or that I would click with someone on an emotional level and develop a friendship that extended beyond the work environment. Instead, work began to evolve, becoming a daily ordeal—eight hours that tried my patience. The coarse edges of stress pounded against my mind as resentment surged around inside me day after day. Because of my physical state, the slightest stressful situation would cause anger to rise up inside of me.

On top of that, I felt misunderstood. Even after months of fighting the fatigue, insomnia, anxiety, and loneliness, no one at work knew what I was going through. When they would view my manner of response to a question or comment as if I was trying to be mean or irresponsible, my insides would suffer even more. My heart would cry out, saying, *You don't understand!*

And then, there was hate.

Someone at my work seemed to go out of their way to bother me. They seemed to do everything possible to stress me out, and I felt as if everything they did caused my situation to get worse. So, I eventually allowed hatefulness to sink in. The bitterness crept into my heart, and I unwittingly accepted it. I began to allow anger to linger, wishing that they would just get what they deserved. At the time, I could not see exactly what I was allowing to happen. Because of my situation, I felt justified in holding onto resentment, but it would take a little while before I could see how wrong I was.

The worst part of the whole situation was not necessarily the sickness or loneliness. It wasn't the stress or the anger. The worst part was what happened between God and me. You might have guessed that all this was happening because I had allowed a rift to occur between me and God. You may have guessed that I had fallen away, decided to stop seeking Him, or became involved in some sort of terrible sin.

If you guessed this, then you would be wrong. In my mind, the worst part about the whole situation was that I was still living for God the best way that I knew how. Yet, He let it all happen anyway. He let the sickness build. Many times, I even felt like He was purposely keeping people away from me so that the loneliness would grow. I felt like He had chosen to place that person in my work environment specifically where they could do the most damage. When I stepped back and looked at the situation, the only explanation I could postulate was that God had caused my pain and misery, despite my efforts to seek Him.

I knew this couldn't be the case. It wasn't possible! I argued with myself day and night. God wouldn't allow all this to happen if I was really righteous before Him! Because of these thoughts, I began to question my righteousness in Jesus. I began to think that perhaps I had lost hold of it and that my sin had finally caught up with me. So, as doubt surfaced in my heart, I once again began to attempt to reach perfection on my own. I once again wrestled with the thought, *If I can get good enough, then I will finally be forgiven. Then, all this pain will go away.*

In my efforts to be more righteous, I started denying myself entertainment and opportunities. I began to think that maybe, if I allowed myself to get to a pitiful enough state, God would finally decide to have mercy and relent. I thought, *If I just don't sin for a long enough period of time, God will see that I've gotten better, and then He can heal me.*

You see, I thought God was mad at me. I knew He must be. It was obvious that I had done something that sent Him over the edge, so He finally snapped and was sending the full brunt of His wrath at me. In my sorrow, I could not see that I had also allowed doubt a place in my heart.

The time I spent alone in that apartment was by far the worst experience I had ever faced in my life. I wanted more than anything for my life to go back to the way it had once been. I wanted God to look somewhere else—at someone else. I still read the Bible, and I still prayed, and I still waited for Him, but it didn't seem to help. Behind many of the actions I performed *for* God, existed a bitterness that I had built up *toward* God. I wanted Him to fix my situation, but I didn't really want to get closer to Him. I reasoned that He had allowed my suffering, and so I had a right to keep Him at arm's length. I placed a halt on my relationship with Him because I thought He just wanted to hurt me more. It didn't start out that way, though. For the first several months, I continued to seek Him with all my heart. In fact, through a large portion of the sickness, I was placing my trust in the belief that He would come through for me. When I reached the point where I felt like I had been completely abandoned, though, I finally started to give in to doubt. It seemed like God had chosen not to do anything about my situation, and that eventually made me mad.

If I could have changed my situation, I would have changed it in a second. If I had been able to, I would have taken myself straight out of that place of pain. Now, as I look back, I can see the solution to my problems. If you're thinking, *Please tell me what the solution is, because I'm in a similar situation*, then you may not like my answer. The whole reason I could not accept the solution during the pain was because I did not like the answer either. My problem was not physical in nature. The big issue I was facing was an attitude problem—I was having a problem with control.

I would have changed my situation if I could have. Jesus, on the other hand, went through a much worse situation. The difference was that He could have changed His situation at any moment, but He chose not to. He went all the way to the cross because God had asked Him to do so. He died for the sins of the world because He desired to do the will of God. I had allowed myself become so angry because of what God had done to me, and yet the whole time I could have avoided a lot of anger and frustration if I had just known one truth: we can't expect God to *bless* us and not *test* us.

I went into that period of my life thinking that God was going to bless me because I was living for Him. I thought that everything would be easy because I was filled with His Holy Spirit. I thought everything would be going my way—yep.

That was it.

I was trying to live *God's way* while expecting everything to go *my way*.

This brings us back to a statement I made at the very beginning of this book: God was going to complete what He planned on accomplishing, and I could get in on it if I wanted to. Unfortunately, I still assumed that God would bend His plans to fit my own. I never for a moment thought that my life would be headed down such a gloomy path. When Proverbs 3:5-6 talks about God leading us down straight paths, I assumed that meant He would be leading me down easy paths. However, God's view of the right path can be different than our own. Does that mean that

God doesn't listen to our prayers or cries for help? No. I believe God hears the prayers of His children. Our attitude toward God should be one of complete and total surrender.

We should be able to say, *God, I'm all in for Your kingdom. I am believing that You are going to provide for my every need, but I also understand that there may be suffering along this path. Even if I have to go through difficult situations, I'll be okay, because I know that You are walking with me. Despite what I see around me, I still believe that Your plans are good.*

I had yet to adopt this perspective. As I sat on that apartment floor, crying uncontrollably, I realized that I was walking through the middle of a dark valley, and there wasn't any getting out of it. There wasn't any going around it. But then, on a day when my fatigue reached its climax, and when I felt more alone than I ever had in my life, hope suddenly found me.

I had been spending so much of my time and effort trying to get out of the valley that I had forgotten to look around in the valley. When I finally stopped squirming and banging my head against the wall, I looked around, and I realized that I was not alone. Someone else had been there the whole time, even when I had doubted His presence.

As I lay on the floor, I made the decision to give up—my dreams, desires, goals, plans, agenda—anything that was keeping God from accomplishing everything He wanted to do in me and through my life. I decided that, if God was allowing me to suffer, then He had a good reason for doing so. I accepted His will over my life, despite my ability to understand it. So, in this moment of release, I began to pray.

Up to that point, I had been praying, *God, do something! I'm begging You to change my situation!* Now, I prayed in my heart, *God, if this is what You have for me to walk through, then I'm willing to continue walking. Your will be done.* When I finally stopped yelling at Jesus to lift me out of the valley, I found Jesus in the valley.

As the words left my lips, I suddenly became filled with the power and presence of the Holy Spirit. It was as if Jesus Himself had stepped in the room with me. I don't think I had ever felt His presence so strong. In my mind, the Lord placed a picture of a valley—a rough, dark, rocky pass between two mountains. I saw myself standing on the road, refusing to go any further, and then I clearly saw an image of Jesus standing a few feet up the path. I could see that He was waving me on, encouraging me to keep walking. I said out loud, "Hey, what are You doing down here?" I opened my eyes as the picture faded from my mind. Suddenly, the voice of the Holy Spirit spoke loud and clear in my spirit. He replied, *Walking with you. I said I would never leave you nor forsake you. So if you're going through the valley, then I'm going through the valley too.*

I found Jesus in the valley, and it changed my life. I had met with Jesus when everything was going my way. I had followed Him and trusted Him when life had been easy, but this was different. In a state of relief, I sat down before Him and just listened. The whole time, I had been Martha (Luke 10:38-42), who had tried to fix everything, prepare everything, and get everything in order. I was doing it all for good reasons, thinking that God would use me if I could just set things right. If I could just figure everything out and get my life back on track, I thought I would be in line with God's purpose. What I had failed to realize was that I should have been more like Mary. If I had just sat at His feet and listened, Jesus would have been able to teach me what I needed to learn much quicker. Jesus says it clearly in Luke 10:41-42.

"But the Lord answered and said to her, 'Martha, Martha, you are worried and bothered about so many things; but only one thing is necessary, for Mary has chosen the good part, which shall not be taken away from her.'"

Mary didn't worry about getting everything together. She didn't worry about trying to fix the situation and make sure everything was going to turn out all right. Mary simply sat at the feet of Jesus and listened.

I wanted to live out God's will in my own way. I assumed things were going to be easy, so when they weren't, I became angry with God. Instead, I should have simply submitted to His plan, which had been at work the whole time. I was so focused on getting my plans back on track that I failed to see what God was doing. Even though I resisted at first, God was still willing to use me for His purpose. In fact, He began to use me right in the middle of the storm. When I hit my weakest point, I finally handed the reigns over to Jesus Christ. As I said, "Your will be done," God began to act.

I began to sit before Jesus at home every day, but at work I sat at my computer, creating videos filled with a message of hope in Jesus Christ. Some opportunities at my job opened up to allow me to begin working on some short ministry videos. I was taking sermon snippets from the well-known Christian leader I worked for and presenting them in creative ways. As I began to create these pieces of art that proclaimed the message of Jesus' saving work, I realized that I was editing the exact messages I needed to hear. These videos were posted online, and comments started to appear from people who had been going through valleys of their own. The first time I read through a string of comments, it became clear that God had a reason—a purpose for my situation.

At the time, I could not see it, but God was also preparing me for other avenues of influence. Now, I have the opportunity to also work on my own ministry videos on my personal YouTube channel. The videos found on that channel all started with an idea that was birthed during my walk through the valley. It was during that same time of hardship that I also started writing the first edition of this book. Now, years later, I can look back and see how incredible God's plan really was. I didn't like it at the time, but it was worth surrendering completely to His plan. I know now that I would not go back and change that time even if I could.

When I finally took the hand of Jesus Christ saying, *I'm going to walk with You no matter where You lead me,* God started using me to help bring hope to others who were facing similar situations to my own. I think many of us want God to put us in amazing situations so that we can do amazing things. The truth is, He used me in a terrible situation to do amazing things. Looking back, I can now see that God was changing my point of view so that He could use me. God had prepared me to do some work that could only be done from the place of impact I found myself at. So, the next time you are in the valley, ask yourself this question: *If Jesus went for a walk through the valley, would I follow Him?* Or do you think God only lives on the mountaintops?

- *12* -

A Divine Healing

My time in the valley, though it certainly tested me, also proved to be a learning opportunity. As I placed the remainder of my hope in the Lord, He began to develop my character. It was during this trying time that several truths from the Word of God became lodged in my heart. These truths were no longer simply ideas on a page; the Holy Spirit was engraining them into my being. I am going to spend a large portion of the remainder of this book talking about those truths. However, first I need to tell you about how God healed me.

Even though I had found Jesus in the valley, I was still *in* the valley. I still battled sickness, loneliness, pain, and anger. The difference was that I no longer faced these hardships alone because I knew that Jesus was with me and because I once again trusted resolutely in the fact that His blood covered me and made me fully righteous, I allowed myself to make a familiar mistake. I assumed that I would immediately be swept back to where I wanted to be.

This, however, was not necessarily the case. Praying day after day, I asked God to heal me and deliver me from my adversity, and I waited patiently for a response. Eventually, the Holy Spirit gently informed me He still had some things to show me. This definitely was not what I wanted to hear, but I chose to trust that God's plan would turn out better than my own. At this point, I chose to willingly stay in the valley and walk with Him no matter what came my way. My patience was rewarded because God did

110

begin to reveal many truths from His Word. He taught me things that I had not been able to fully learn while climbing up the mountaintops or skipping through the plains.

The truths that He began to teach me were simple lessons I had read in the Bible several times over. However, because of the trials I faced, and because I had no where else to place my hope, His words were suddenly made real to me in brand new ways. As I began to hear His voice and sense His hand at work in my life. My hope was restored, and I knew that God still had good things in store.

A pastor sat at one of the empty, old church pews after service one Sunday. The congregation had cleared out already, leaving him alone in the quiet sanctuary. He had delivered a heart-wrenching sermon about trusting in God, but he himself was questioning God's willingness to help him overcome the trying circumstances he faced in his own life. As his eyes dampened, he prayed, "God, my life is falling apart. I keep reminding the people in this church to trust You, yet I can't seem to get over my own fear of failure. I keep telling these people that You are going to be there when their marriages get tough, but I feel like my own marriage is out of control. I keep reminding them that You are their provider, but the church's finances are plummeting, and I don't know if we'll recover. I keep showing people in Your Word how You desire to heal them, but I don't see how You could possibly heal the cancer I'm facing."

Only a few seconds passed before the still voice of God spoke to his troubled spirit. The Holy Spirit gently whispered, *I've got it.*

"You've got it?" the man asked with overwhelming frustration. "Did You not hear all of the things I just said? You saying, 'I've got it' isn't going to fix anything! I thought You were supposed to be there for me! How could You have let all of this stuff happen?"

He leapt up and walked out of the room, furious at God's nonchalant response to his prayers. He stormed outside, discovering that his youngest daughter was already waiting in the car for him to take her home. As he sat down in the driver's seat, he looked back, seeing tears in his daughter's eyes. "Honey, what's wrong?" he asked.

She looked up at him with reddened cheeks and said, "Daddy, my life is falling apart." The pastor smiled inside at the fact that his daughter was making such a big deal over the little troubles she was facing. He knew she had not even begun to experience life. "The kids in class keep making fun of me because of my hair," she said. "And the teacher keeps pointing out when I mess up the memory verse."

The pastor looked kindly at his daughter and said, "I'll take care of it."

Then, drying her tears and forming a smile on her face, she looked back at him and said, "Okay." The pastor was silent for a few seconds, and then told his daughter that he had forgotten something in the church. He headed back inside, walked down the aisle, fell to his knees next to the same pew as before, and simply said, "Okay."

A child is willing to trust that, no matter how big the circumstance may seem, his or her daddy is bigger. No matter how bad the situation may be, his or her daddy has things under control. When we come before God as His forgiven, redeemed children and say, *God, it looks like I'm not going to make it through this. My life is falling apart. Help me.* God says, *I've got it.*

Let me tell you from experience, when God says He's got it, you can believe that He does. I'm not saying that God's answer is always going to be the one we're looking for, but I am saying that God is never going to lose control of the situation. He's never going to be surprised by your issues. The waves during the storm on the sea were not too big for Jesus to calm then, and the waves in your life are not too big for God to calm now.

The problem that we often face is not in hearing that God has got it but in believing that God has got it. Listen to what Jesus says about belief in Mark 10:15:

"Truly I say to you, whoever does not receive the kingdom of God like a child will not enter it at all."

We spend so much time trying to enter the kingdom of God (or interact in the kingdom of God) on our own that we forget how God really wants us to enter. Some people strain so hard to enter the kingdom of God through their own intelligence and intellect that they pass up the only door available.

God has not called us to solve our way into His family. There's no magic formula to unlock the keys of the kingdom of God. It's not possible to manipulate our way into His presence. He simply told us to trust in His Son like a child would. This means that we take Him at His word. It means being willing to become vulnerable and admit that we don't have it all together. It means being willing to put everything on the line and step out in a faith that doesn't always make sense.

Look what God has to say about our human wisdom in Isaiah 29:14 and 1 Corinthians 1:19:

"Therefore behold, I will once again deal marvelously with this people, wondrously marvelous; and the wisdom of their wise men will perish, and the discernment of their discerning men will be concealed."

"I will destroy the wisdom of the wise, and the cleverness of the clever I will set aside."

Trying to figure out—and therefore, control—God only leads to frustration. Attempting to receive the benefits of the kingdom apart from entering and operating on His terms only leads to disappointment. When we try it our way, we wind up becoming irritated, and cynicism starts to eat away at our hearts. The more we try to follow God our own way, the more we think that He has let us down, and this way of thinking only breeds doubt. If we do things our own way too long, we can eventually get to the place where we doubt if He even loves us at all.

Fortunately, God has plainly stated the answer to our doubts. As I stated earlier, I believe that you are reading this book for a reason. I don't believe that you started reading on accident. If you can receive it, this is what I believe God is saying to you right now: *Trust Me the way a child trusts a loving parent. Trust Me with all your heart.*

Instead of trusting Him though, we often inch our way along, making sure that each piece of ground we walk on seems stable before we tread on it. If we're doing this, then we've missed the fact that God does not always work on stable ground. He often works in the midst of turmoil because He wants you and me to understand that He *is* our stable ground. When it seems like everything is falling apart, God is still active. If God is ever going to do something great in our lives, we first have to be willing for Him to take us to a place of vulnerability. We have to be willing to be molded by Him.

Being molded by Him requires us to actively respond to trials and opportunities in faith. God provides the faith, but we are commissioned to actuate it through our choices and beliefs. When we're not willing to use the faith that God has given us, we quickly grow dormant. It's easy to end up wondering why God isn't doing anything, but it's not always easy to accept the fact that God has already called us to do something. He has called us to respond to His words in faith.

The most intelligent person can read the Bible and hear the verse that says we must become like children, yet they can completely miss what God is saying if they trust solely in their own intelligence. If God told us not to lean on our own understanding, why do we assume we can understand how God operates if we simply study Him long enough? We orchestrate whole church services based off of the idea that if we perform just right God will respond, but we can still miss out on finding God because we are not willing to lay our pride aside and run to Him like children. To connect with God's wisdom, we have to be willing to lay our own wisdom aside and just accept what God has said, no matter how silly it may sound at times. Either God is God, or He's not.

One time, a man was talking with a coworker that attended the same church. He said, "Man, you won't believe what happened last night. I met with God. It was wonderful. It was like He was right there with me. Every worry and frustration faded away, and there was nothing left standing between me and Him."

The coworker replied, "Wow. That service last night was pretty good, but I didn't realize it was that good."

The first man replied, "Oh, I didn't make it to the service. My car broke down half way there."

I want you to ask yourself a prying question: are you allowing your pastor or worship leaders to call on God for you? A child doesn't have to go over to a friend's house and ask their friend permission to get their own dad's attention. They simply go to their father and say, "Dad, I've messed up. I need your help."

Isn't that what we do though? We hang out at church, watching the festivities, thinking that God is interested in our attendance. God doesn't want you at His church. He wants you at His feet. He doesn't want your attendance. He wants your brokenness. If you can give God your brokenness, it isn't hard to give Him everything else. When we come before Him, vulnerable and broken, and confess that we cannot do it on our own, He reaches down, picks us up, and says, *Then come walk with Me, and let's see what we can do together.*

It is said that when you get in a car crash, it is better to relax than to tense up. However, most people's first instinct in a crash is to stiffen up. The same goes with life. When our lives are on a downward spiral and we are about to crash, we do our best to hold everything together, thinking that we will somehow reduce the damage. I would not be surprised to find God asking the question, *What are you doing? Do you really think that is going to help?*

What we don't realize is that all of us are in the middle of one big crash. Apart from Christ, all of our lives are slowly heading toward a collapse. If we never call out to God, then no amount of preparation is going to help. We can't do it. We cannot hold life together on our own—we cannot save ourselves. That is why God has said, "...*whoever does not receive the kingdom of God like a child will not enter it at all.*" He wants us to relax and fall at His feet.

Relax your tensions. Relax your efforts. Relax yourself. The problem with relaxing is that it means giving Him control, and we don't want to let God have control because that would mean us losing control. And that isn't something we want to lose. The truth, though, is that God is much better at keeping things together than we are. Even when everything does fall apart, He is able to put it back together. Relaxing in His presence takes trust, and trust takes childlikeness.

I keep talking about God's good plan—a plan that I assumed was going to make me happy. As I started working after college, this was the hardest aspect of God's wisdom for me to grasp. Reading verses like Romans 8:28 and Jeremiah 29:11, I made the assumption that I would naturally think God's plan was good when I saw it. The issue I quickly ran into was that God's version of "good" varied from my version of what was "good." God does have good plans in store for His children, but His idea of good is not always going to directly correspond with ours.

Here's the key that finally helped me accept the difference: His plans are good, and they are also better. Trusting in God doesn't always mean that life is going to look good to you. It means that you are willing to let things happen His way, even when it's not what you necessarily desired. I know that's not an easy thing to do, however, I can personally testify that it's worth doing. It's worth taking the position of child and allowing your heavenly Father to take the position of Daddy. His wisdom, His goodness, and His love working together to shape your future is never a bad thing.

One time, three men shipwrecked a small boat on a deserted island. They had limited provisions of water but no food. After several days, the men began to grow intensely hungry. One night, they gathered together and prayed that God would send them food. After they fell asleep, God appeared to each of them in a dream and said that He would send a supply of food the next day. All they had to do was wait for it. When they awoke, they discussed the correlating dreams and agreed that God had really said He would send them food.

The first man readied his harpoon and looked out to sea. The other two asked him what he was doing, and he replied, "I'm waiting for the shark that God is going to send. I don't want to miss it so I'm preparing to kill it as soon as it's near."

The second man lifted his bow and arrow up toward the sky. The other two asked him what he was doing, and he replied, "I'm waiting for the birds that God is going to send. I don't want to miss them so I'm preparing to shoot them as soon as they fly over."

The third man set down his fork and knife and gave out a large burp. The other two asked him what he was doing, and he replied, "I just finished eating the steak that God sent."

When we're unwilling to approach God in an attitude of childlikeness, we make ourselves into the first and second man on the island. When we reject the childlike frame of mind that God has asked of us, our intelligence begins to lead. Here's what our intelligence (apart from the wisdom of God) is always going to tell us: *you need to work harder to please God.* We think, *God may have said "Just believe" but He really meant "Just believe and also do all this other stuff on top of it."* I'm not saying that God wants us to sit around and do nothing. If His Spirit is living inside of us, He will lead us into faith-filled action. I'm saying that we can do nothing apart from abiding in Christ (see John 15:5), and abiding in Him requires an ongoing childlike belief in His finished work on the cross.

God has certainly called us to do His work, but we cannot work if we're not walking with Him. We cannot begin to please God apart from the blood of His Son, Jesus Christ. If you're stuck in an endless cycle of self-effort in an attempt to please God, you may need to come back to the start and ask yourself the question: *Have I truly believed that Jesus did everything at the cross?* If the answer is no, I encourage you to read what Jesus says about self-justification in Luke 18:9-17. The first step to a fully surrendered trust is a willingness to come before God humbly—to come to Him the way a child would.

The idea that we cannot enter God's kingdom apart from becoming children should definitely shake us up. Here's another thought that ought to shake you up; if we had to become like children in order to enter the kingdom, then how do we expect to function inside the kingdom apart from continuing to be childlike? Some of us give God our brokenness when we're in a bind, but when we begin to feel a restored sense of peace, we once again pretend like we have it all together. We once again go to church, sing songs, act spiritual, and forget that God still desires our hearts and not only our actions. *Why doesn't God desire our actions?* He does, but the heart always comes first. If He could ever get your heart beating for Him, He knows your actions would follow.

There is a kind, amazingly loving God who desires your heart. He wants to see you free, blessed, filled with His Spirit, and functioning at your top capacity in His kingdom. He wants to do good things—great things—in your life. Believe that He is who He says He is. Believe that He is going to do what He says He is going to do. Don't let anything stop you from believing. Don't let other people get in your way to God. Don't let your circumstances tell you when you can or cannot rest in the presence of Jesus Christ. Don't let your intelligence stop you from fully receiving the grace of God in your life today. Trusting God with your whole heart may seem impossible at the moment, but don't worry. Jesus said in Luke 11:9-12:

"So I say to you, ask, and it will be given to you; seek, and you will find; knock, and it will be opened to you. For everyone who asks, receives; and he who seeks, finds; and to him who knocks, it will be opened. Now suppose one of you fathers is asked by his son for a fish; he will not give him a snake instead of a fish, will he? Or if he is asked for an egg, he will not give him a scorpion, will he?"

If you want to believe God, ask Him to help you believe Him. If you want faith to trust God fully, ask Him for it. He is faithful, and He will provide. Stop worrying and ask. Good things are in store. Believe it.

Do you believe God hears us when we ask for things? I do. I want to share a specific time when He heard my prayers for help. I told you earlier that I was going to tell you how God healed me. I do have to admit, it didn't happen the first time I prayed. For God's good reason, that I could not see at the time, I prayed many times before I was suddenly healed. One night, I was lying before God asking Him to heal me when I heard His voice in my spirit. He asked, *Do you believe that I can heal you?*

I answered, "Yes, I believe that you can heal me."

Then He asked, *Do you believe that I will heal you?*

I didn't give myself enough time to doubt whether or not He was going to heal me, so I quickly answered, "Yes, I believe You are going to heal me."

Then He said, *As you believe, so will it be done to you.* At that very moment, I felt a physical change in my body and I knew that I was healed. As the weeks passed after that, the pain that had left my body that night did not return.

I was healed because I asked to be healed. I asked because I believed. When I asked, God heard me. Like I said, it wasn't the first time that I asked. I didn't just sit down one day, ask to be healed, and then everything suddenly went back into place. I sought God. God had a reason for the valley I was going through. He was teaching me several things, and one of those things was that I had to believe that He was actually going to heal me when I asked Him to heal me. During that same time, I had been reading about all the people who asked Jesus to heal them in the Bible. Jesus sometimes asked people if they believed He could do it. Like those who Jesus healed in the gospels, I also had to lay down my fears and frustrations. I had to surrender my logic and, like a child, trust that God was going to hear the voice of His kid.

Since that day, there have been multiple occasions in which God has healed me after I asked in faith. One time, while I was spending the night at my parents' house, I was suffering from a severe ache in my left leg and hip. My leg and hip had randomly started to hurt two days prior, and the pain slowly increased until it was no longer bearable. I had to hobble around during the day, and I was in so much pain that I could not fall asleep at night. I lay there on the bed, writhing in agony, hoping that the dawn would come. Nothing helped. I thought I was simply going to have to live with the pain. Then, I realized that the answer was right next to me. My Bible sat on the shelf next to the bed, and in it, I had just been reading about the story of Jesus and the blind beggar. The account goes like this in Mark 10:46-52:

"Then they came to Jericho. And as He was leaving Jericho with His disciples and a large crowd, a blind beggar named Bartimaeus, the son of Timaeus, was sitting by the road. When he heard that it was Jesus the Nazarene, he began to cry out and say, 'Jesus, Son of David, have mercy on me!' Many were sternly telling him to be quiet, but he kept crying out all the more, 'Son of David, have mercy on me!' And Jesus stopped and said, 'Call him here.' So they called the blind man, saying to him, 'Take courage, stand up! He is calling for you.' Throwing aside his cloak, he jumped up and came to Jesus. And answering him, Jesus said, 'What do you want Me to do for you' And the blind man said to Him, 'Rabboni, I want to regain my sight!' And Jesus said to him, 'Go; your faith has made you well.' Immediately he regained his sight and began following Him on the road."

I had just been reading this story of Jesus and the blind beggar not just a few hours before I once again lay in pain, hoping that something good would happen. As I remembered the faith of the beggar, I decided that it was time to use some faith of my own. I crawled out of bed and hobbled through the house. It was difficult just to make it to the door. I put on my shoes, all the while feeling the cringing effects of movement. I didn't stop there. I went outside in the middle of the night, and I walked up the hill in front of my parents' house. I stepped out onto the old country road that runs past their house, and I began to wobble down it. I took a step with my good leg, and then I took a step with my not-so-good leg.

Each step hurt, profusely, but I didn't quit—neither did Bartimaeus. When he shouted, the people rebuked him. When the people rebuked him, he shouted out even more. I continued to hobble down the long, sloped drive, until I finally came to an intersection at the bottom of a hill about a quarter mile down the road from the house. Halting next to a stop sign, I knelt down at the end of the road. Looking up to heaven, I shouted, "Jesus! Son of David! Have mercy on me!"

Wow. You were pretty desperate. If that's what you're thinking, you would be right. My actions were also based in something more solid than desperation though. I knew what the blind beggar knew. The blind beggar knew who Jesus was. He had heard of Jesus and everything He was doing. He had heard stories of all the people Jesus was healing, and he knew this was his chance. He believed that Jesus could heal him, and because he believed it, he wasn't about to let Him pass by without a fight. You know, Jesus didn't have to heal Bartimaeus that day. If Bartimaeus had not cried out, Jesus would have simply walked on by, and Bartimaeus probably would have remained blind for the rest of his life. However, Bartimaeus knew who Jesus was, and because of His belief, He cried out. Remembering the faith of Bartimaeus, I knelt down, as painful as kneeling was, and I cried out. I shouted into the darkness, "Jesus! Son of David! Have mercy on me!"

Out in the night, I could see nothing but trees, clouds, and road, but guess what. The darkness shouted back! It said, *Be quiet. Jesus has better things to do than deal with your pain. He's got hurting people on the other side of the world that need to be healed, so let Him worry about them.* It was the voice in my own head telling me that Jesus wasn't motivated enough to heal me. I believe those menacing thoughts originated from a spirit of doubt brought on by the enemy. After all, Satan could see everything I was doing. He could hear my shouting into the darkness the same way God heard me. He knew I meant business, so he quickly sent thoughts my way that said, *Jesus is too busy. He isn't going to listen to you.* As soon as I heard the thoughts, I knew they were from the devil. I knew they were nothing more than a lie. You want to know how I knew? I knew they were lies because I knew Jesus.

I believed that Jesus was who He said He was in the Bible. Despite the lingering thoughts, I believed He was going to heal me, so I continued to shout even louder. I yelled out, "Jesus! Son of David! Have mercy on me!"

Then, knowing that God had heard me, I waited. When the beggar cried out, what did Jesus do? It says that Jesus said, "Call him here." When Jesus calls you, you know you are in a good position—you can bet that something great is about to happen. As I knelt there, I heard the gentle voice of God in my spirit. The Holy Spirit asked, *What do you want Me to do for you?*

I answered, "Jesus, I want to see," which meant, "I want to be healed." God understood what I meant, and He knew what I needed. He could see my need the whole time, but He waited for me to trust Him before moving on my behalf.

Bartimaeus could have remained silent and let Jesus pass on by, and he may have regretted it for the rest of his life. I called to Him because I believed Jesus cared about me just as much as He cared about Barimaeus. When I said, "Jesus, I want to see. I want to be healed," Jesus said to me, *Run home.*

I let out a gasp. "Run home?" I asked. "You've got to be kidding me." I waited for a while longer, and then I felt the voice of the Holy Spirit stirring me once more.

He asked, *Do you want to be healed?*

I replied, "Yes, Lord."

And He said, *Run home.*

I complained, "Lord, I can hardly even hobble, and You want me to run?"

God replied, *Yes.* I sat there, thinking there had to be another way. Then I heard it again, *Run home.*

I heard it over and over in my spirit until finally I said, "Okay. It doesn't make any sense to me. I could hardly walk down here, but since You say to run home, I'm going to run home."

Struggling to my feet, I turned around and faced the steep hill that lay before me. It was nearly pitch black, and it would be difficult to see where I would be going, but God had said, *Run home.* So, to the best of my ability, I ran. I took one step, and the pain surged through my leg and up into my hip. I ignored it. I took a second stride. The pain surged again, bringing a tear from my eye. Still, I continued to trust that God was going to do what He said He would do. I continued to trust that God was telling the truth. I took a third step, and the pain was gone. I took a fourth step, and the pain was gone. I took a fifth step, and the pain was still gone. It was gone. I began to jump around, trying to find the pain. I tried to recreate that burning feeling, doing everything I could to make it come back. I leapt back and forth and ran in circles. The pain was *completely* gone.

Bartimaeus was told, "Take courage, stand up! He is calling for you." His response is amazing: "Throwing aside his cloak, he jumped up and came to Jesus." Bartimaeus believed that Jesus could really heal him, so he didn't hesitate to run to Him. You may not realize it, but he was also acting out of faith when he threw aside his cloak. His cloak was what he had used for so many years to cover his body as he sat there, so he normally would have been extra careful not to lose it. He may have even laid it before himself to collect money as he begged, but his actions show he believed he didn't need it anymore.

As I began to run, it was as if I also threw aside my cloak. My actions were saying, *Jesus, I believe You can and will heal me. I believe that You care about me. I believe You are telling the truth.*

What did Jesus say to Bartimaeus after He healed him? He said, "Your faith has made you well." I wasn't healed because I was running. I was running because I believe I would be healed. My actions stemmed from the fact that I believed God was going to heal me like He said He would. If you are in pain and you need a miracle from God, I encourage you to stop sitting on the roadside wondering if anything is ever going to change. It's time to step out in faith. It's time to start believing that God desires to heal you. It's time to run to Jesus.

In Exodus, the Israelites received a great deliverance from God. God led them out of Egypt and across the Red Sea unharmed by Pharaoh's army. You would think they would have been pumped up with faith, but they quickly forget what God had just done. Upon reaching Mount Sinai, they turned their backs on God and began to worship a golden calf. They were acting as if they had delivered themselves—as if they had not just witnessed a miraculous work of God.

Even when we see God work in our lives, sometimes a heartbeat is all we need to forget what He's done. As I was about half way up the road, a thought suddenly crossed my mind. I thought to myself, "What a strange coincidence." Can you believe it? I had just received a miraculous healing from God, and I let the thought enter my mind that it may have been nothing more than a coincidence. The miracle was sitting there right before me, and I doubted.

It's a good thing that God is right there to lift us back up again when we repent. Thomas doubted, but Jesus extended His amazing grace to His friend and disciple. I received that same grace. Though for a moment I doubted the work of God, God continued to fill me with His Spirit, and He reaffirmed the work that He had done. It's a good thing God is faithful, even when we are not. It's also amazing that God loves us, even when we doubt it.

If you need healing, call out to Him. If you need a miracle, has He heard you telling Him about it? Speak it to Him—pray constantly. Remember though, He hears you every single time you open your mouth. He hears every word you speak, no matter how loud or how quiet, and no matter how often you say it. God hears you. Believe that He is who He says He is, and believe that He is going to do what He says He is going to do.

- *13* -

Making It Out Of
The Valley

I didn't just wake up one day and think, *Oh boy, I've made it through the valley*. But God did give me knowledge about when my circumstances were going to change. I believe God is going to do one of two things when you ask Him to deliver you in faith. He is either going to pick you up out of the pit right then and there, or He is going to speak into your life and give you a promise to hold onto. When you come before God in humility and cry out for Him to save you, He hears you. We see this beautifully stated in Psalm 10:17:

"O Lord, You have heard the desire of the humble; You will strengthen their heart, You will incline Your ear."

He sees you, and He cares. When you cry out to Him in faith, believing in Jesus for your righteousness, He is not just going to sit there and watch you suffer. Psalm 34:19 speaks of God's response to the righteous person in need:

"Many are the afflictions of the righteous, But the Lord delivers him out of them all."

Now, I'm not saying that God's response is always going to look exactly the way we want it to. Remember, His wisdom is greater than ours. Also, if you do not know God and you are simply crying out in order to justify your suffering, then God may just let you suffer until you admit that He is the only One who can deliver you. But when you cry out to God in faith, knowing that He is the only One who can truly save you, He will answer you in His love. This is what God did for me as I trudged through the worst of muck. As I crawled through a barren wasteland, I began to cry out to God every day, and He heard me. He began to reminded me of His goodness and His plan, which was already in effect. His presence showed up, and He put Himself in the midst of my problem. He further revealed Himself and His ways known to me as the intimacy of our relationship deepened.

When I first began to cry out to God, after months of suffering through lonesomeness and sickness, God began to show me where I was. He painted a picture in my mind of the valley in which I was situated. As I lay before Him with tears in my eyes, I could see the mountains that surrounded me. I could see the trees and the hills. I could see the shadows and the fog. I could even see the muck in which my feet seemed to be stuck. However, as I said before, I could see Jesus right there with me.

If you belong to God, He is never going to let you go through a trial or a test alone. He will never walk away and watch you go through something by yourself. He may step back just enough to see if you will fall in His direction, but He will never leave you alone. No matter how difficult the circumstance may seem, He will always be there, ready to catch you. As I began to seek God, I realized how close He really was. I could see Him standing there in the muck with me, pointing out which direction to go.

Months went by—months that seemed to eat away at me. I felt like I was falling apart. I felt like there was nothing left that I could do to hang on, but something inside me drove me on to seek the Lord; something inside me gave me courage to follow after Him. Then, one day, I was given another picture. These pictures were obviously nothing more than metaphors of where I was situated in life, but the Lord knew they were what I needed during that time.

As I lay before God, I found myself at the bottom of an incline. There were rocky cliffs on both sides, but at the very top was an opening, and I could just make out a ray of light shining down into the darkness which surrounded me. God was saying, *You're almost there.* That hill that lay before me was the last stride. It was the final step that I had to conquer before I made my way out of the valley. The best part about it was that, even though I couldn't see it, I knew what was on the other side.

I knew that I still had a while to go, but God had filled me with hope. However, it was up to me to receive that hope. I could have told myself that I was just imagining things to make myself feel better—that God had not really given me these illustrations to hold onto. But, as I prayed, I could feel His presence so strongly, and I chose to believe that He was actually speaking to me. You see, I'm a visual learner. Some people are programed for auditory learning, and others for hands-on learning. God knows how He made you. I believe that God is going to speak to everyone differently, and I believe He was speaking to me the way I would hear Him the clearest.

As I continued to dig into His Word, God brought me the Scriptures I needed in order to keep walking. God brought me the encouragement and peace I needed to continue. He still had a goal and purpose for me, and my life was not going to end in the valley. If you have made it this far, then I have something to tell you. God is not done with you. God has a purpose for you, and it's far more important than anything you have had to go through to get to it. He is going to use you. Even after everything you have faced, He is still going to use you.

Stop thinking that you are going to meet your end in the valley. Your road does not end here. It does not end where you are. God is taking you down the narrow road, and sometimes that means you have to walk through the valley that most people aren't willing to walk through. But when you get to the other side, God is going to unfold a plan that is beyond anything you could have ever imagined for yourself. God isn't about to be done with you, so don't give up on yourself. And when you feel like falling over, fall in His direction. He is always going to be there to catch you, and when God catches you, you can expect a loving embrace.

When God catches you, you get so caught up in His love and goodness that your circumstances suddenly seem like nothing. God is a big God, and He has good plans for you. Don't let a test stop you from reaching the goal. Don't let a valley stop you from reaching the end of the road, which is eternal life and peace in Jesus Christ. The really good news is that you can have that same life and peace right now. You don't have to wait until you reach the end of the road. In belief, ask God to fill you with His peace, and He will do it. Ask God to fill you with His life, and He will do it. Trust Him. Seek Him. Find Him. Because when you find God, you will discover that the valley is nothing in comparison with Him. God is everything, and everything else is like a whiff of cloud. God is in control, and everything in creation falls under His Lordship. Trust Him. He's got you. David wrote in Psalm 23:4:

"Even though I walk through the valley of the shadow of death, I fear no evil, for You are with me; Your rod and Your staff, they comfort me."

But I still don't deserve for God to comfort me! I don't deserve for Him to be my rescuer! If that idea is still plaguing your thoughts, let me set your mind at ease. You're absolutely right.

Here's how to rectify that fear: none of us deserve for God to rescue us. Look back at the fall of man for a moment. Imagine for a minute that we were all taking a boat ride with God across a raging sea. God suddenly said to us, *Don't get too close to the side of the boat, because you may fall out. Those waves you see: that's sin, and I know it's going to drown you if you fall into it.* But in our rebelliousness, we decided to leap out into the stormy water. We wanted to know what the water felt like, but we quickly found ourselves drowning, struggling for life. Would we deserve for God to save us? Not at all. However, in His great mercy and love, He too leapt out of the boat. He firmly grasped us, lifted our head above the water, and pushed up back up into the boat, He Himself drowning in the process. You see, the fall of man was us jumping out of the boat. Jesus hanging on the cross was God diving in after us.

No, you don't deserve for God to be your rescuer, but He did it anyway. Jesus did not die for you because you deserve it; He died for you because God loves you. He chose to love you because that's who He is. God is love. If Jesus came despite how much you did not deserve Him, then you can trust that God still wants to be your rescuer today, no matter how much you think you don't deserve it. He even tells us this in His Word in Romans 8:32:

"He who did not spare His own Son, but delivered Him over for us all, how will He not also with Him freely give us all things?"

After it seemed like I had been in the valley forever, God gave me a third and final picture. I could see myself walking up the hill that led out of the valley. I made it over the final hill, and now I was standing in a green field. In that place of comfort, I found out what David was talking about in Psalm 23:2 when he said:

"He makes me lie down in green pastures; He leads me beside quiet waters."

In the picture the Lord gave me, the dew was fresh upon the grass, and the wind was blowing. A single tree stood in the middle of the field, and next to it was Jesus. He reached out His hand and said, *You made it.* At that moment, I knew that the valley was behind me. I had heard Jesus say this same phrase once before, and I'll share it at the end of this book. But this time when He said it, I knew that I had been brought to a new place. I knew that something new lay before me, and I believed that God was opening up His arms and releasing a blessing upon me that only His loving wisdom could design.

- *14* -

What God Taught Me In The Valley

JOY

Near the beginning of this book, I told you that I wanted to relate the story of my mess. I found myself in two major messes during the first several years of my adult life. The first mess I caused myself. I gave myself over to the lure of sin, thinking that, because I held a place of favoritism with God, I would be able to "get away" with a few slip ups. Instead, I found myself whirling down an unstoppable drain called sinful living. However, in my despair and desperation, I finally realized my need for a Savior, and I called out to Jesus.

The second mess I faced was one of a different nature. The trials of isolation, loneliness, and fatigue felt at the time like an impassable valley. However, through the mess, God reached in and changed my heart once more. As I came out the other side, I could clearly see His hand at work, and I began to trust in His good work in my life. I had learned to value His desires over my own, even when I could not understand what He was doing.

So, for the remainder of this book, I want to share with you some of the specific lessons I learned during my time in the valley. I didn't write this book because I think I'm better than anyone else—I know I'm not. However, I also know that all followers of Christ are saved by grace, and we're all in a process of becoming more like our Savior. Because we've all been through different trials, I believe God can use all believers to build each other up. That is what I hope the final chapters in this book will do for you.

The first thing I want to talk about that I learned while struggling through the valley is this: God is the source of true joy, and His joy will sustain us through thick and thin. Joy is not an emotional state. Rather, it is a conditioning of the heart, centered in hope, and brought about by God's Holy Spirit. Sometimes I forget to be joyful simply because of how difficult everything seems at the moment. There are moments when I'm too hard on myself, and I tell myself that I don't have any joy because I haven't done enough for God or because I have failed to do something I was supposed to do. When I step back and allow the Lord to correct me, I find that the truth is very different. The main reason we lack joy is because we lack His Spirit. The reason we lack His Spirit is because we don't believe. If that throws you for a loop, allow me to explain.

Joy is a fruit of the Spirit, and the fruit of the Spirit accompany the Holy Spirit, Himself. So, when we are abiding in Christ, operating in His presence, and being led by His Spirit, we get to experience the fruits that come from that nearness. How then do we receive the Spirit? Do you remember what Jesus says we had to do to receive the Holy Spirit in Luke 11:9-13? He simply says, "Ask."

If it's so easy for believers to ask in faith and receive the Holy Spirit, a promise from God made by Jesus Himself, then why don't we operate in the Spirit more often? I believe it's because we don't ask, and we don't ask because we're not really believing that it's that simple. Here's the key: if Jesus said it, you can believe it. You can believe it because God's character is one of pure truth—He does not lie. How can you trust His character? Look at what He did for you on the cross. You can believe His words because He already demonstrated His true nature on the cross. Jesus said, "God so loved the world," and then He backed up His words by dying on a cross for a sinful world. You can trust God when He says that He wants to give good gifts to His children. He's already given His very own Son.

If you are in need of joy, where should you start? Pray and ask for the Holy Spirit, then simply wait in His presence. When you stop thinking of everything you have to do, when you stop focusing on the waves that are pounding against you, and when you stop thinking that perhaps you aren't going to make it, and you begin to focus on Jesus Christ in the midst of everything, your joy will overflow. Your joy will overflow because the Holy Spirit will manifest Himself in you and give you a reason to rejoice. Romans 14:17 states:

"For the kingdom of God is not eating and drinking, but righteousness and peace and joy in the Holy Spirit."

Without His Spirit, we can be momentarily happy, but we cannot possibly have true joy. Without His Spirit, we cannot be filled with the joy of the Lord, which is the source of our strength as believers.

Don't we often attend church or read the Bible seeking joy? We seek joy because our lives are filled with junk that can hit us from every angle. We think, *If I can just find some joy or peace in this situation, I will make it through.* The worst part about it all is that we remember the joy we once experienced. At one time we had that joy that we are seeking. It dwelt in us and carried us. It fed us and wept with us.

But there are times when the joy has been taken and the forces of heaven and earth seem to join against us, working to steal any sort of hope we may have left. If you are facing anything like this, it's time to get that joy back. *How? I tried! I tried to get the joy back and I've failed. It eludes me at every turn. It's like it doesn't want to be found.* The reason it feels like it doesn't want to be found is that you cannot find it on your own. Joy isn't something to be discovered or happened upon. It isn't something that wells up inside of you when you reach a certain level of spiritual maturity. Joy is a fruit of the Holy Spirit. But instead of seeking God—instead of seeking His Holy Spirit—we seek joy, and we wonder why we don't find it. If you're having a hard time accepting this, read 1 Corinthians 2:14:

"But a natural man does not accept the things of the Spirit of God, for they are foolishness to him; and he cannot understand them, because they are spiritually appraised."

If you're having a hard time accepting a truth from God's Word, ask God to make it ring true for you. Ask Him to help you appraise it spiritually. The promises of God don't always sound reasonable to our flesh. To receive a gift from God, our old nature tells us that we have to do enough for God, but God promises joy to those who are abiding in Him—walking by the Spirit. God wants to give you joy, and He wants to deliver it through the presence of His Spirit. You can believe it.

Let me tell you about my friend. No, I'm not talking about Jesus, though He is the best friend anyone could ask for. I'm talking about my friend Luis, who I first met during my sophomore year of college. Luis and I could go anywhere and do anything. As long as we were together, we knew that we would be okay. To say that we were best friends would be an understatement. In fact, I'm convinced that Luis is the type of friend who would do anything for me. During school, if I were in trouble, I knew I could count on him to come to my aid. Anytime we hung out, I didn't worry about anything because I knew Luis was there. When Luis was there, I had reason to rejoice.

At the moment, Luis and I are living in two different countries. Let's say one day I decide that I am going to recreate that feeling of friendship, security, and joy that I had while he was with me. So, what do I do? Imagine with me for a moment that I take out a picture of Luis and carry it around with me everywhere I go. Anytime anything comes up that I can't handle on my own, I turn to the picture of Luis and say, "Luis, you've got my back on this right?" That would be crazy. Holding a picture of my friend is not the same as having the real person with me.

Some of us go to church, sing songs to God, and pray because we want to create a feeling of hope that only the real person of Jesus Christ can give us. We're willing to walk through the steps if it will help us feel better, but we're willing to lay everything down. Some of us want to know the joy of the Lord without knowing the Lord. I have people ask me often how to be filled with the Holy Spirit and how to receive the fruits of the Spirit. Guess what; the answer is not a magic formula. The Bible does tell us to ask in faith, but we need to remember that God is not a puzzle waiting for us to figure Him out. He's a person, and He's waiting for us to seek after Him with our whole hearts. When we are whole-heartedly pursuing Him, we're going to find Him, and that's when His Spirit and His joy are going to fill our lives.

"Then Jesus said to His disciples, 'If anyone wishes to come after Me, he must deny himself, and take up his cross and follow Me.'"

Matthew 16:24

We are happy to watch Jesus carry His cross, but it's a different story when it comes to picking up our own and following Him. Picking up one's cross does not mean saving one's self. Jesus already paid the full price for our sin. Instead, it is a sign of complete surrender to God. It is a sign of submission to Him. It is a sign of belief. You see, in order to really leave everything behind and pick up one's cross, you and I must first believe. If we don't believe that what God says is true, then we aren't going pick up a cross. If we're still hanging on to our doubts, then we aren't going to follow Him. We are simply going to stand there, staring at our cross, wondering why Jesus is leaving. It's easy to desire the benefits of God, but the benefits don't apply unless we accept the calling of God. When we cry out, *God! I need some joy! I need some peace in my life,* I believe God says, *Come, walk with Me. Pick up your cross and follow Me. It's not always going to be easy, but If you're walking with Me, I'll provide all the joy you'll ever need.*

Now, let's suppose that one day Luis said to me, "Troy, no matter what problem you are facing, I will help you get out of it." Because he is my trusted friend, I would believe him. Let's also say that the only way I could convey the problem to him was to literally hand it to him. Guess what? Because I believed what he said, I would get on a plane, take a car, ride in a train, or do whatever I needed to do to get to where he was. When you truly believe something as amazing as the perfect gift of righteousness through Christ, you are not going to let anything stop you from getting it. The reason we have a hard time exchanging our problems for joy in the arms of Jesus is that we are still standing right where we were when He called us. Jesus said, *Follow Me*, and we said, *Anywhere, Lord*. However, years later, we are still considering the cost of getting up and going after Him.

Listen, I know this can be a hard thing to hear, and I'm not saying that every believer is in this place. You may be following the Lord diligently. You may be seeking Him with all your heart, and if so, that's awesome. You may be on the other side of the fence, though. You might be saying, *I've lost too much time*, or *I'll never catch up to where I am supposed to be*. The truth is none of us have fully followed Him like we should have—none of us have done this perfectly. The good news is that Jesus has not called the righteous, but sinners (Luke 5:32). Jesus may feel far away, but remember that He's near to those who call upon Him. Now is the perfect moment to say, *Lord, I've messed up. I didn't do what I was supposed to do. I strayed, Lord. I left the path. I didn't follow You. I wanted to, and I even tried to part of the time, but stuff got in the way and I let it keep me from finding You. Help me.* When you call out to Him, Jesus will meet you where you are. He will meet you right here.

I believe that Jesus is saying, *It's time to shake off the chains that have held you down. It's time to let loose the cares that have slowed you up. It's time to take Me at My word and begin to truly believe that I am going to do what I say I am going to do. There is a path that I have called you to. Yes, it's not the easiest path. Yes, it will cause you to give up everything, but the pursuit is worth it. It's worth it because of the promise I have made to you about where you are headed. When you stumble, I will be there to lift you up. When you falter, I will be there to hold you steady. I will fill you with abundant joy and peace, and I will provide for all of your needs. Put your trust in Me, and let's go.*

This is what I believe Jesus is saying right now. He's asking you to seek Him with your whole heart and to not look back. There is a hope we have in Jesus that is greater than anything we could ever face, but it's up to us to let go of our own desires or fears and begin to look at Him. The world is never going to satisfy, but Jesus always lives up to His promises. The world is going make claims that it can never follow through with, but you can trust that Jesus is going to make good His word to you.

You might be asking, *What promises are you talking about?* Here are a few of God's promises to His children:

"And we know that God causes all things to work together for good to those who love God, to those who are called according to His purpose."

Romans 8:28

"And He has said to me, 'My grace is sufficient for you, for power is perfected in weakness.'"

2 Corinthians 12:9a

"Do not let your heart be troubled; believe in God, believe also in Me. In My Father's house are many dwelling places; if it were not so, I would have told you; for I go to prepare a place for you. If I go and prepare a place for you, I will come again and receive you to Myself, that where I am, there you may be also."

John 14:1-3

"He who did not spare His own Son, but delivered Him over for us all, how will He not also with Him freely give us all things?"

Romans 8:32

These are some amazing verses, but don't let this be your source of God's promises to you. Please don't. Don't be satisfied with me telling you what God has in store for you. That's like letting a friend read a love letter intended for you and then having him or her translate the important parts over to you. Go read it for yourself. God has promised so many amazing things; go read them for yourself in His Word. Once you begin to understand the promises that He has spoken, you will begin to see just how great of a journey He has in store for you. Once you begin to understand that we are not just living for the temporary, you will truly begin living. God has a master plan—a great goal ahead. He has an idea for your life that will rock your world.

Don't do that! Not today! Don't start thinking I'm talking about someone else. Don't start thinking I'm talking about that highly intelligent, God-fearing, perfect Christian that sits on the front row in church. God has a plan for *you*—messed up, hurting, imperfect *you*. And it's a good plan. It's so fulfilling that you could not even begin to understand it at the moment.

Unfortunately, there are two things that can get in the way of God's plan. No matter who you are, if you are a believer, there is a calling that has been placed on your life, but two things potentially stop you from fulfilling it. The first is this: you don't really believe that God has good plans for you. How often do we listen to that voice that's telling us that God doesn't know what He's doing? The problem is, once we start doubting God's good plan, the paths of our lives become a confusing labyrinth—a maze of options. In the end, we end up settling for less than the best because we aren't receiving the divine leading that God intended for us to have on our journey. The good news is this: you can know that God has a plan for your life. In Isaiah 49:23, God makes a promise to His chosen people. He says:

"Kings will be your guardians, And their princesses your nurses. They will bow down to you with their faces to the earth and lick the dust of your feet; and you will know that I am the Lord; those who hopefully wait for Me will not be put to shame."

If you are a believer in Jesus, you have been grafted in to the olive tree, which is simply a way of saying that God considers you one of His chosen people. That means that you can take the principle found in this verse and apply it directly to your life. When you wait hopefully on God, you will not be put to shame—your life won't be wasted. If you choose to wait upon the Lord, you can't fail. Will the world see you as a success? Not necessarily. However, you'll be a success in God's eyes, and that's far more important. When we wait on Him and allow Him to change our hearts, He sets us on the path that He has in store for us.

I want to look back at one of the verses that started me on the path toward the Lord. I'm talking about Jeremiah 29:11-13. Now, I understand that this verse has been used out of context in so many ways, however, I still believe it's applicable to our lives today when we look at it from the correct perspective. God says to His people:

"For I know the plans that I have for you,' declares the Lord, 'plans for welfare and not for calamity to give you a future and a hope. Then you will call upon Me and come and pray to Me, and I will listen to you. You will seek Me and find Me when you search for Me with all your heart."

What does this mean for us? Like I said before, if you are a believer, you can apply the principle from this verse to your own life. After all, God is the same yesterday, today, and forever (see Hebrews 13:8). If God had good plans for His people in the Old Testament, then He has good plans for His people now. However, here's the biggest way I believe this verse has been misused: God's good plans don't always look like our good plans. We want God to have our own "good plans" in store for us, and we want to reap the benefits of those plans simply by quoting verses like this one from Jeremiah.

That truth is that God does have good plans, but they are *His* plans—not ours. God's path for your life is not always going to look easy. He doesn't guarantee that you'll be rich. He doesn't promise that you won't suffer loss. He simply promises that you won't be disappointed (and I'm not talking about your flesh being gratified). He promises to listen to us when we call out to Him, and He promises that we will find Him when we search for Him with all we have.

In the end, it comes down to you believing Him enough to seek Him. The plans He has for you are amazing because you get to walk with Him during the journey. If you will seek Him with all your heart, you will find Him, and He will make His plans known to you. Believe me, He is worth everything you have to give up to pursue Him.

That leads me to the other thing that can stand in the way of God's plans for your life: *your* plans are still in effect. It's so easy to say, *God, I want to seek You,* but then allow our time to be eaten up by fleeting pleasures. It's easy to think, *Here's my heart, God,* but then dwell on our own desires. Some of us are never going to find Him and His plans because we don't want to give up our own. When you step back and look at it from the perspective of eternity, God's plans really are the only ones that matter.

Yes. I agree with you in theory, but you don't understand how bad I want this other thing. I mean, I really, really want it. I want it so bad that I can't even image not having it. If I gave it up, I have this deep feeling down inside me that I'm not going to be able to do without it. I know what you mean. How do I know what this feeling is like? I know because I have the same feelings. There are dreams, goals, and wishes that I have that I feel like I could never live without completing. There are things that I feel like I must do and there is no other way around it. But when I first began to lay those desires down in front of my King, He did something amazing. He took that space that had once been filled with dreams of mine, and He filled it with dreams of His own. He took my potential and multiplied it. He took my desires and formed them into something lasting. Many of my deepest desires have never truly begun to be fulfilled until I completely gave them up.

God Himself has actually placed a lot of your deepest desires in your heart. Now, because of the sin nature, we are born with desires that are not from God, and we can be set free from those desires by the power of Jesus in our lives. However, many of our good desires come directly from God. If we seek to fulfill those desires on our own, we are just going to wind up empty, wondering why our dreams did not satisfy.

As you seek God, allowing Him to be the master of your desires, He is going to fill you with Himself. He is going to complete everything that needs to be completed in you, and in the process, He is going to make you whole. My deepest prayer now is that God would simply give me His desires—that I would want what He wants, and that He would empower me to follow after Him.

A question is raised when I start pondering God's calling on my life: what does my purpose look like practically? If you've ever asked the same question, I believe Ephesians 4:1 gives us the answer. It starts out by saying:

"I, the prisoner of the Lord, implore you to walk in a manner worthy of the calling with which you have been called."

Then, verse 11 says:

"And He gave some as apostles, and some as prophets, and some as evangelists, and some as pastors and teachers, for the equipping of the saints for the work of service, to the building up of the body of Christ."

It's talking about our calling as believers in Christ. If you have received Jesus as your Lord, there is a work of service that He is going to lead you toward, and the purpose behind the work is to build up the body of Christ.

I believe there are two ways we can build up the body: by inviting people in, and by strengthening those who are already members. In short, if you're wondering what your calling looks like, ask yourself this question: am I seeking to win souls and encourage believers, or am I just seeking to better my position in life? I know we all have unique, God-given purposes, but if we're actually allowing the Lord to lead us, our purpose is always going to be working toward our common goal as followers of Christ. I encourage you to examine the practical, day-to-day aspects of what you believe God is calling you to do. If your "calling" never gets around to building up the body of Christ, then it's not from God. Remember though, our work should be motivated by the love of God, not a sense of duty. If you're asking God what your calling is right now, I encourage you to start there: ask God to solidify your identity in His love for you.

If you remember where we started in this chapter, you may be thinking, *What does all this have to do with joy?* I have said all this to say one thing: apart from fulfilling your God-given purpose, it is impossible to truly know the joy of the Lord. God has put you in the situation you are in to complete a calling that He has placed on your life. He has called you to great things, and He gives you His Holy Spirit to help you follow His leading. Joy is a fruit of the Spirit. If you are not listening to the Spirit and allow Him to work through you, His joy will be hard to come by. How do you know the work that God has called you to do? How do you know your purpose? You find your purpose by finding Him. Once you find Him, He will fill you with His presence and all the love, joy, peace, patience, kindness, goodness, gentleness, faithfulness, and self-control that you need. You will have everything you need in Him. Find Him, and you will find a joy that is the very strength that sustains you. It will sustain you as you continue taking the next step down the narrow road.

I have experienced the most joy during some of the saddest times in my life. I know that sounds crazy, but think about it like this: when you lose an animal that you care about, perhaps your dog named Sparky, you are sad. Though this sadness may feel overwhelming at the time, you know that things will get better. Eventually, you will not look back and remember how sad you were when Sparky died, but instead you will remember all the good times you had with your furry friend. You will laugh, saying, "Remember the time when Sparky…"

You may face hard times in your life, but when you are walking with Jesus, that hard time is only a stage leading to something better. When you look back, you will not think about how difficult that time was, but instead you will see a life of friendship with your Maker. Unlike Sparky, you don't have to worry about Jesus dying. He already did, and He came back so that you wouldn't have to face those hard times alone. You will be able to say, "Lord, remember when you got me through that mess?" Joy is centered in hope. Our hope is centered in Jesus and His amazing love for us.

FORGIVENESS

One of the best ways to free yourself is to free someone else through genuine forgiveness. During my walk through the valley, I began to feel encroaching feelings of hatred toward several people in my life. Some people that I worked with were beginning to annoy me as I went into work each day. I felt like they were purposefully trying to make me feel out of place and unwanted. And added to that were my thoughts: *You have no idea what I'm going through outside the job right now. You have no right to treat me this way. You just have no right!*

So, day after day, my feelings of hatred would grow. They blossomed until I would even feel the weight of the emotions physically affecting my body. At the same time, feelings of anger began to grow against my family; I felt like they had abandoned me. My feelings were not really justified considering how little I had told them of my situation, but they were there nonetheless. I felt like they should have done or said something.

I felt deserted, by everyone and anyone I had known. And this feeling caused the anger to expand. As the hate accumulated, I slowly added more and more people to the list of those whom I had something against. I slowly hated more and more of my friends and family for doing nothing about my situation. The worst part about it was that I could hardly even tell who my anger was directed at.

I was simply angry. I was angry at the world, and I was unsure why. I knew it wasn't anyone else's fault that I had come to be in such trying circumstances, but the anger grew nonetheless. And this thought led me to hate one more person. I reasoned, *If I'm in this situation because I was attempting to do what God wanted me to do, then God is responsible for me being here.* And this made me hate Him even though I was diligently seeking Him every day. I was doing what I thought God had called me to do at that time, and yet my situation kept getting worse and worse.

When you begin to hate God, your source of joy and peace immediately goes out the window. When you begin to walk around all the time with a grudge against the Creator of the universe, you are in for a sorry time. I'm not saying God is going to all of a sudden start throwing everything He can at you because you are angry with Him, but you will lose the benefits of loving God. You will lose the benefits of being filled with the joy and peace of His Holy Spirit. I would ask God for His Spirit, then directly turn around and shake my fist at Him for what He did to me. Or I would praise Him one moment and then grind my teeth at Him the next. I knew I was justified by faith, so I thought I shouldn't have been experiencing what I was experiencing. But I had missed two very important facts.

God had a plan, and I had forgotten that. I was so worried about getting out of my situation that I couldn't see God's reason for having me in the situation. I couldn't see His perspective. I had covered my eyes to His love. Also, though I was complaining that God should treat me better since I was justified by faith, I wasn't really living by faith. I was living every moment scared that I wouldn't find a way out. I had forgotten that God has called us to believe and trust Him in *every* situation. Instead of being miserable and sulking about never being able to change my circumstances, I should have trusted God in the midst of my circumstances.

Sometimes, having faith means allowing God to do something you would not have thought of. I would never have put myself in that situation, but thank goodness God's ways are higher than my ways. God put me there for a reason, and He waited until I chose to act out of faith to show me what that reason was. God was in the process of doing something amazing, yet I wouldn't stop being angry with Him because He wasn't doing what I wanted Him to do.

So, what did I do about it? Not much. I simply asked God to change my attitude, and He did. Though unable to understand how angry I was at Him and everyone else, I still cried out to Him. I still believed that He could do all things. I still believed that He loved me, despite my situation. I wasn't able to see His love at the moment, but I still believed that it was there. I knew that God had sent His Son Jesus to die for us because of His great love, and so I looked to Jesus. I had little evidence of His love for me in my surroundings, and so I had to focus on what Jesus did at the cross. If God loved me enough to send His only Son, I knew He loved me enough to bring me through my situation and to do something amazing at the same time. It took me a long time to get to this point. Once I began to believe, God began to act. Once I began to look at my situation through the lens of God's promise, He began to move.

One night, I sat in on a service led by Pastor Chip Ingram. He was talking about forgiveness. This was right after I began asking God to change my attitude. I knew I was angry, but I could not figure out how to escape the anger. What God did was remind me that one of the best ways to free one's self is through forgiveness. Chip told the story of a person he had to forgive earlier in his life. He said that it was difficult at first, and he sometimes wanted to go back to hating them, but with God's help he was able to walk through the process.

I included this because I want to remind you what God can do through a simple sermon. I know some of the things I have said could possibly lead you away from church or from Christian circles, but God is a big God, and if you are seeking Him, He will meet you no matter where you are. When you go to church, believe that God is going to speak to your situation. When you sit at home, believe that God is going to speak to your situation. And when you go out to eat with friends or family, still believe that God is going to speak to your situation. God is going to speak to you, if you will seek His face.

And that is what He did that night. He spoke to me in my situation. I was so lost in anger that I didn't even realize I needed to forgive those around me. I began to list the names of those I was harboring anger towards. Then, I gave those names to God and said silently, *God, I know it's not going to be easy to forgive, but I'm going to do it anyway. I'm trusting that You will help me do it.* God suddenly brought up several names I would never have thought of on my own. God even reminded me of people from my past— people like the girl in high school who had hurt me. I thought, *Do I really need to forgive these people?*

You can never forgive too much, and one crazy thing about forgiveness is that it usually never makes sense. We always want to wait for people to come groveling at our feet before we will even think about forgiving them. But when you forgive your brother from your heart—before they even ask—God will do something incredible for you in your situation. That is what He did for me. As I transferred people from the begrudged section in my mind to the forgiven section, I began to be healed. As I let go of the bitterness, the anger went with it.

It's one thing to say you forgive someone in your heart; it's another thing to actually go and treat them like they are forgiven. It's a process— one that the Holy Spirit will lead you through. Every time a hurtful comment or remark would surface, I would feel the anger swelling up again, and then God would remind me in my spirit that I had spoken forgiveness toward that person. I had chosen to take on the forgiveness of Christ, and so once again I would choose to let it go.

That night when Chip Ingram spoke, he said that forgiveness wasn't just a one-time deal. It was continual. As I attempted to walk the road of forgiveness, I discovered exactly what he meant. Just because you forgive someone doesn't mean they are going to change automatically. Along with forgiving someone, pray for them as well. Pray that God will work in their life and that He will bless them. *Bless them? Are you serious?* Yes. You may not want them to be blessed, but pray it anyway. Jesus even asked God to not hold His murderers' sin against them, and I believe that's the kind of forgiveness God desires us to replicate. Ask God to bless them, and in the process, God will hear you about your own situation as well.

I was learning to forgive those who I felt had harmed me, but there was one other person that I needed to forgive. I still had anger in my heart toward God. I still resented His presence. I thought, *God, you've brought me this far, but I think I can handle it on my own from here. I don't want to be around You, because Your presence reminds me of what You did to me. You remind me of what You allowed to happen.* You may be thinking, *Do we really need to forgive God? He is perfect and He never makes mistakes.* You are right. God does not make mistakes, but we don't always understand His ways. His ways are perfect, but we can't always see why. What I mean by forgiving God is reminding yourself that He has your best interest at heart. I'm talking about letting go of the bitterness.

Forgiveness involves changing the way you treat someone. If we really believe that God loves us, then we are going to lay our anger down and say, *God, I thank You for everything You have put me through, because even when I can't see it, I know that You have a plan for me that is far beyond any plan I could make for myself. I know that You love me, and I know that You want what is best for me.*

When you are willing to lay your anger down at His feet and treat Him as one you have forgiven, you can begin to praise Him in the midst of difficulty. God sometimes lets us face tragedies so that we do not become tragedies. His beautiful plan will unfold in the end, but we have to believe Him enough to accept what He gives us. We have to believe Him enough to continuously ask for deliverance and freedom. God is going to do it, if you will believe it. Once you believe it, you won't be able to help but to see God through a lens of love and thankfulness.

Let me remind you of something: God knows all of our hearts. He continuously hears the complaints, the whining, the rejection, and the hatred of people's hearts, yet He still sent His Son Jesus to take upon Himself everything we deserved. If you are angry with God, remember what He went through so that we wouldn't have to face His anger. When He was angry with His children, He gave up everything so that we would not have to feel His wrath. Can we not take the example that Jesus set for us and also forgive those who have harmed us? Can we not learn from Him and love one another? Forgiveness is a process, and it's one that God will walk with you through. Rely on His strength, His capability, and His companionship. And forgive. When you set someone else free, you really set yourself free.

PATIENCE

As I walked through the valley, God also taught me that I could practice patience in Him—even while battling a barricade of anger and confusion. Anger will tell you that you have no reason to praise God. It will attempt to point your eyes at the mess you find yourself in and tell you that the difficulties justify your resentment toward God. It will even tell you that God doesn't care, if you let it. Anger is not intrinsically a sin, but it can lead to sin when you allow it to pry your trust away from God.

When you get angry, you have an opportunity. You have an opportunity for development and intimacy. *What on earth are you talking about?* We were designed to worship God—to praise Him.

The Bible says we were created for His good pleasure (Philippians 2:13, Revelation 4:11). The very being who is God deserves praise no matter what, simply because He is God. His existence constitutes one who is deserving of our praise. On top of that, God demonstrated His amazing love toward us by sending His Son to die for the sins of the world. So, God is deserving of our praise because of who He is and also because of what He's done. However, no matter how deserving God is, anger still finds a way to convince us that God is not worth praising.

It's easy to praise Him when times are good, but most of the time that means we are praising Him *because* times are good. When times are bad, and I mean really bad—when your life is falling apart and anger seems to be taking over—there's only one thing to do: praise God. *What?* Praise God. Praise God for who He is, and praise God for what He's done. *Why?*

The devil will point to your emotions and attempt to persuade you that God is undeserving of praise, but the Word of God says otherwise. When we choose to believe what the Word says about God's character—that He is good, loving, and gracious—despite our feelings, we take a leap of faith. The Bible tells us that the Lord inhabits the praises of His people (Psalm 22:3). So, if you're praising Him in Spirit and in truth, He's there.

The Bible also tells us that freedom follows the Spirit of the Lord (2 Corinthians 3:17). So, if praises invite the Holy Spirit in, and the Holy Spirit issues freedom, then the reason the devil doesn't want you to praise God is because he doesn't want you to be set free. He wants to keep you caged in by your raging emotions, but God desires to give you victory over your emotions and liberty to react to your emotions in a healthy way.

The major truth we see in God's Word about praise is that God deserves it. When we take the time, even in our anger, to praise God and say, *God, You are worthy of adoration simply because of who You are*, then we allow God into a private area of our lives that most people think He's too judgmental to see. The biggest fear I've had when it comes to talking to God about emotional battles is what He might say about my issues, but when we open up about our struggles with God, we give Him the sign that we desire true intimacy with Him. Yes, He does often correct our wrong behavior, but He does it lovingly—with a heart of grace. God doesn't want us to pretend like we're okay if we're not—He desires us to be honest. Being honest with God takes trust, but it also builds trust because we have to lay it all down and believe that God truly is who He says He is—that He really does love us, and that He deserves all praise.

When you give your anger to God, He begins to gently work on your heart. He takes your emotional highs and lows and transforms them into passion for His Kingdom. He transforms the heart that you allow Him to become a part of.

When we give God our worst state, He reminds us of His worst state. He reminds us of the day when Jesus hung on the cross for you and me. His closeness reminds us of His deep and unending love for us. His love turns anger into a Godly passion. It transforms helplessness into wholeness. It fills empty hearts. It fixes our messed-up lives and our messed-up attitudes, and it redeems that which has been lost.

Patience isn't something we were born into. It is something we have to learn, and God understands that. Learning to be patient means learning to change *you*. It means allowing God to change who you are. If God says, *Not today,* our first response should be, *Thank You, Lord* and not, *When, Lord?* When you are stuck in a rut, and there seems to be no way out, adopting this attitude may seem impossible. However, the more we allow the Lord to grow patience inside of us, the more it becomes our default reaction.

Let me remind you of an individual that God used for mighty deeds who at one point in his life seemed to be heading nowhere. I'm talking about King David. The thing about David you have to keep in mind is that he wasn't always a king. At one point in time, his job was to hang out in the fields all day watching sheep. If you look at God's plan for David's life, it's clear to see that David was not a sheepherder; David was a king. But before he could realize his kingship, he first had to herd some sheep.

God has a good plan in mind for you—He is going to do something great in your life, if you let Him. If you stop focusing on the situation you are in, and begin to focus on Him, He will bring you to the place He has already prepared for you. It's not always going to look the way you want it to look, but it's going to be good. How do I know? Simple. God is good (Psalm 100:5). It's in His nature to make good plans. We're not always going to understand His ways—sometimes we have to trust that God's version of good really is good—but as we learn to be led by His Spirit, we are going to be able to praise Him no matter where He takes us.

David spent a good deal of time out in the fields with no one to keep him company but a bunch of sheep. It may seem like you are spending a lot of time hanging around sheep; but let me tell you, when God begins to do what He is going to do, you are going to thank Him for the time you got to spend with the sheep. When David was out there with the sheep, he was also out there with God. Listen to what God thinks about David in 1 Samuel 13:14. Samuel says:

"The Lord has sought out for Himself a man after His own heart, and the Lord has appointed him as ruler over His people."

God knew David. David knew God. David and God knew each other. David didn't pretend to know God so that he would feel good about himself or so that someone else would view him in a better light. David actually *knew* God. David knew God because he sought God's heart. Remember how I said patience is not something we are born into? It is also something we cannot learn on our own, but when we begin to grow close to God, developing that intimate relationship with Him, He will begin to change our hearts. He will give us the patience we need, but it's up to us to respond to His love.

If God has dropped you out in the field with the sheep, then He is saying, *Seek Me.* He is saying, *Seek Me, and find Me.* God desires us to seek Him with all our hearts, but we often focus so much on the sheep, the mud, the rain, or the rocky landscape that we forget to seek Him. When we get to heaven and God asks us what we were doing with all the time He gave us, what are we going to say? *But God, there were rocks out there! There were stinky sheep, mud, grime, and hard times.* God may just respond, *Was all that more important than Me? Were the setbacks you faced more powerful than Me? If you had sought Me, then I would have been there as well—right in the middle of it! When I showed up, none of that other stuff would have continued to matter.*

When God is there—when the Spirit of the Lord is present—the circumstances that normally try to tear us down suddenly become nothing. It's easy to get so frustrated wanting to be somewhere else doing something else that we miss out on the gorgeous opportunity God has given us right now. If God has you watching sheep at the moment, you can trust that He's got something much better planned down the road. But if you spend all your time complaining about where He has put you now, why would He want to take you someplace else? God knows that if you aren't seeking Him where you are, you aren't going to be seeking Him where you wish you were. We have to get to the point where we desire the presence of God over a change in our circumstances. God isn't going to test you to see if you can work hard enough to find your destiny. He's going to test you to see if you will seek Him no matter what.

I believe that one of the worst things you can do to a human is to force them to waste their time. This is why we look at waiting on God as something to be done while at church. We may think, *Well, I'm already wasting two hours of my day anyway, so I should at least give some of this time to God.* But the truth is this: waiting on God can be the best use of our time, if we truly learn to wait. God desires us to be patient, but more importantly He desires to impart His divine patience to us. Patience is a fruit of the Spirit, so without the Spirit, true patience cannot exist. When we attempt to wait on our own, the anger and frustration and confusion take over. They overpower us. But 1 John 4:4 says that:

"…greater is He who is in you than he who is in the world."

If God is in you, and I'm talking about the indwelling of the Holy Spirit, then there is no amount of anger that can overcome you. There is no level of emotional adversity that can prevail. There is no test that can beat you.

The question that could be raised is: *does God really test us?* I believe the answer is *yes.* James 1:2-7 says this:

"Consider it all joy, my brethren, when you encounter various trials, knowing that the testing of your faith produces endurance. And let endurance have its perfect result, so that you may be perfect and complete, lacking in nothing. But if any of you lacks wisdom, let him ask of God, who gives to all generously and without reproach, and it will be given to him. But he must ask in faith without any doubting, for the one who doubts is like the surf of the sea, driven and tossed by the wind. For that man ought not to expect that he will receive anything from the Lord."

James makes it clear that tests will come. God tests us so that perseverance will develop inside of us, because He desires us to mature spiritually. God has a good plan for you and me, but if we never reach the level of maturity that it would take for us to handle that plan, then we may never see it progress. *I can't do it. I'm not smart enough to get to that level of spiritual maturity.* What you cannot do, God will do through you. *You* seek *Him.*

God has placed you in the situation you are in so that you will believe Him. James says, "if any of you lacks wisdom, let him ask of God, who gives to all generously..." God lets you face trials so that you will realize just how much you need Him. He will let you get to the point where *your* wisdom fails, so that you realize how much you need *His.* Once you realize how little you have, God will remind you how much He is going to do.

The amazing thing about this whole process is that everything starts with belief, and that's why James tells us to ask in faith. If you never reach the point where you choose to prioritize your childlike belief in God, then James lets us know that you shouldn't expect to receive from God when you ask. I've heard a thousand different ways that people in the church attempt to explain unanswered prayers. Perhaps a lack of childlike belief should be the first reason that comes to our minds. I'm not saying God is going to do everything you want Him to do if you believe. True belief in God means a complete trust placed in His Word.

Anything God said He will do, we can believe He will do—not necessarily anything we say He's going to do.

You want to believe? Read His word. You want to believe? Get in His presence. You want to believe? Ask God for belief. Start with what you've got and then go from there. Use the faith God has already given you and He will give you more. No matter what trial God leads us through, He will always be there to lead us out, if we're willing to put our trust in Him. He will always be there when we call upon Him in faith. He will always show up when we take the time to wait upon Him.

Look at the amazing thing that happens when we believe God's Word enough to spend our time waiting upon Him. Isaiah 40:31 says:

"Yet those who wait for the Lord will gain new strength; they will mount up with wings like eagles, they will run and not get tired, they will walk and not become weary."

God is waiting for us to wait on Him. He is waiting to pour out His Holy Spirit. A fruit of the Spirit is joy, and it's a lot easier to practice patience when you're filled with God's joy. For this reason, I believe that patience and joy go hand-in-hand. But as I stated earlier, true joy won't be present unless the Spirit of God is present. In fact, patience is a fruit of the spirit too, so the same applies to patience. Waiting for something to happen is one thing, but patiently waiting with a joyful attitude is another.

Nehemiah 8:10b says "…the joy of the Lord is your strength." So, what is going to happen when we patiently wait upon God? He is going to fill us with strength that comes from the joy of His Spirit. I don't know about you, but I want to run and not be weary. I want to walk and not faint. If you find yourself still walking through the same swamp you were walking through years ago, then it's time to ask in faith for the joy of the Lord. It's time to wait patiently upon Him, believing that you will receive all you ask for in faith. It's time to be filled with His strength so that you can walk and run with God at your side. There isn't anything that God cannot outrun. If God is running with you, then you've got nothing left to do but hang on. I believe that God is going to do something great in your life, but you've got to wait on Him. That means taking the time to get in His presence. That means being determined to find Him. It means being diligent to prioritize a childlike belief. It means learning patience.

TRUST

I talked about the importance of trust as it relates to patiently waiting on the Lord, but there are other aspects of trust that I also want to talk about. One of the hardest things I've ever had to do is to simply trust God when everything around me is falling apart. When life begins to crumble around us, I believe Satan takes that opportunity to tempt us into settling for a less-than-providential destination. God has a fulfilling goal—a restful purpose—in mind for you, and even though you may not be able to see it at the moment, it is there. When you settle for a worldly offer, you are saying either you don't believe God has something better in store or you are telling Him you just don't want it. I'm talking about opportunities that look good to us, but the Holy Spirit is telling us to pass up.

As the weight of missed opportunities continues to grow, an inclination grows to look for rest and purpose in something other than what God has planned. We think, *I need this*, when all along we didn't really need it. What we need is God. If you are finding it hard to trust God in the midst of a storm, and you feel like you can't wait until later to find rest, then I have some good news: you can rest right now, even in the middle of uncertainty. When you allow the presence of Jesus Christ to flood your life, rest simply happens. We don't have to arrive at our destination to find fulfillment. If we're trusting in the promises of God, and listening to the Holy Spirit, we can be content, fulfilled, and complete right where we are. Instead of seeking something else to fill that void and settling for something that is less than God's all, trust Jesus to give you the rest you need. Jesus said in Matthew 11:28:

"Come to Me, all who are weary and heavy-laden, and I will give you rest."

Resting in God's presence requires us to prioritize our relationship with Christ. It requires us to draw near to Him in faith, trusting that His words are true.

Sometimes, I feel like my Christian walk turns into a lonely marathon. I see my God-given purpose as this massive task that I don't have enough time or resources to complete. When I'm running the race in this state of mind, I always come to a point of collapse, because I was not meant to carry the weight of life on my own. What I forget is that I have a friend in Jesus, and He has asked me to lay my burdens before Him and simply trust. You were not meant to bear your burdens alone. God's not asking you to carry the weight of the world on your shoulders. Jesus carried it on His. If you know Jesus, you get to run the race side-by-side with your Savior, and He is able to lighten your load so that you can keep going. But it's up to you to trust Him—to come into His presence and hand off the weight.

There are many burdens that try to hinder our walk: shame, addiction, depression, fear, anxiety, over-commitment, selfishness, greed, and the list goes on. Some of the burdens we carry are sinful (or guilt left over from sin), and others are not. Either way, Satan will try to use them against you. His goal is to get you to trust the burden more than you trust God. He will tell you that you can't beat that sinful habit because it's too powerful. He will say that you can't win against depression because it's something that runs in the family. He will lie about shame and tell you that you still have a reason to hold onto it.

The truth is that the sacrifice of Jesus lightens our burdens in two ways. First, Jesus bore our sins (1 Peter 2:24), so sin and shame both have to let us go when we trust in the blood of Jesus and apply the power of God's grace to our lives. On top of that, fear no longer has a hold on us because we have been perfected in love (1 John 4:18).

Second, Jesus also bore our griefs and sorrows on the cross (Isaiah 53:4). That means that hardships like depression, emotional highs and lows, and anxiety have to leave when we enter the presence of our Savior. The devil is a liar, but God is ever faithful. His word is relevant, life-giving, and powerful. However, it would be difficult to say that you're trusting in God's Word if you're not reading it. His Word is there for you! Trust Him enough to prioritize it.

One day, I was lying on my bed, thinking about everything I had to do and the fact that I did not feel like doing any of it. In my mind, I could see my responsibilities piling on top of one another and weighing down upon me. I felt the weight so heavily that it made my stomach hurt. Suddenly, God asked me, *Troy, how long does it take you to run around a track?* I was on the track team one year in high school, and sometimes the tension before a big race would cause great pains in my stomach.

I answered, *I could probably go once around in a minute, if I was booking it.*

Then God asked another question. It's funny how God can ask one simple question, and simultaneously answer several of mine. He asked, *How long does it take Me to run around a track?* By the time I could come up with an answer, God would have crossed the finish line. It would take Him no time at all. As I pondered the endlessness of God's ability, I was reminded of 1 Peter 5:7:

"Casting all your anxiety on Him, because He cares for you."

We often try to push through the pain as we carry life's burdens, but the truth is that God desires to carry the load for us. No matter how much we have to transport, and no matter how far we have to go, God can do it in no time. Instead of turning to God for strength, we often turn to worry. When there's no option left, we look to God and say, *Help.* Even if you find yourself in this situation today, it's never too late to set your eyes on the Lord. He is the source of our help, and when we cry out to Him, God says, *Hand Me the baton. It's My turn to run.*

As I journeyed through the valley, every day I would wake up hoping that God would save me—wishing He would take me out of my situation. It's not that I wasn't seeking Him—I cried out to Him about it all the time. I would seek Jesus, but my hope was in the idea that He would take me to a peaceful situation. It was okay to ask for this, but I should have also been trusting Him to give me peace in the situation I was in. I wasn't praying in faith, because at first, I was only viewing my situation through the lens of my own desires. I thought, *God could not have put me in this situation, so His will is obviously to get me out of it. I just need to pray enough and my situation will change.* What I did not realize is that God did put me in that situation, and His will was for me to be there a little longer. I was so focused on *my hurt* that I missed *His plan.* I was so focused on *my comfort* that I missed *His purpose.* God had a greater purpose in mind, and I eventually saw it.

Even though God's temporary plan was for me to walk through a valley, His long-term plan was different. As I continued to seek Him, I finally began to see my hardships from His perspective. As I stood in my kitchen one day, washing dishes in the dark because the light was burnt out, I begin to pray out loud to God. I said, *God, I'm acknowledging the situation I'm in, and I'm admitting that I need your help to walk through it, no matter how long it lasts. I spend so much time trying to ignore it or get away from it that I forget to thank You for bringing me through it and giving me peace at all times.*

I had forgotten that, in Christ, I could have peace in *every* situation, not just during good moments. Because I had forgotten this, I thought I had to jump ahead to the good times to have peace. In His grace, God was showing me that I could have peace right where I was, in the middle of a terrible storm. I could have peace because He was with me. He was protecting me. He was watching out for me.

In fact, what I could not understand at the time was that the storm I was in was the very best place for me to be. It was the exact place where God was going to teach me, and it was in His will for me to be there in that moment. It was where I was going to grow. I learned something very valuable that day: if at any single moment you are doing what God wants you to do—even though there are millions of things in the universe you might rather be doing—at that moment, you are doing the very best thing you can possibly do. It's up to us to trust that God's will is better than our own—to believe that He is good and He has a good reason for everything that He does.

Trust is a process. It doesn't just happen right away. It takes faith, but it also requires an intimate relationship. If you are a believer, God has you in His hand, no matter where you are. If you know Him, then He is always walking next to you, no matter how rocky the path becomes. Jesus said it like this in Matthew 28:20:

"…and lo, I am with you always, even to the end of the age."

If He is with you always, then that means He is right there in the valley with you, even when you don't feel it. If you will learn to trust Him, you can have peace and rest all the time, no matter what may be going on around you. Lasting peace comes when you and I learn to simply rest in His presence, trusting in Him above all else.

HEALING

One of the most unforgettable things I experienced in the valley was the power of God at work in my body. We serve a real and living God, and He is the same yesterday, today, and tomorrow. This means that, the same way Jesus healed all those people in the Bible, He still wants to heal you and I today. Before I get into the reason I believe God still heals, I want to tell you about one of the first times I ever received supernatural healing.

One time when I was in college, in the middle of several weeks of hardcore cheerleading practice, I began to experience a problem with my jaw opening and locking in place. It often happened in the middle of practice, but sometimes it would come on when I was just hanging out and talking. I would open my mouth, and then not be able to close it again. I probably looked as if I were yawning for several minutes. Let me tell you, it was frightening—nerve racking. I lost my ability to swallow, I could no longer communicate, and on top of that, it was painful.

As the cheerleading season progressed, this locked jaw problem began to occur more and more frequently. I guess it happened one too many times though, because it eventually drove me to frustration. One day when my jaw locked open, I got mad. In my irritation, I let go of my fears about praying for healing, and I started talking to God about it. I asked God to heal my jaw, but I did not simply ask Him to fix the issue. I asked Him to heal my jaw completely so that it would never lock up again. This is a dangerous prayer to pray. It's dangerous because immediately the thought comes up, *If it ever comes back, then God either isn't listening to me or doesn't want to heal me—or maybe He doesn't heal at all.* I guess that shows how irritated I was. I prayed in faith, and I didn't care what thoughts might arise. I simply got into the presence of the Lord and asked Him to take it away for good.

To this day, my jaw has not locked up. The day I prayed that prayer was the very last day my jaw ever locked in place. You might be thinking, *Wow.* Or you might be thinking, *That's just a coincidence.* If you're in that second camp, please know that I'm not trying to judge you, however my hope is that you'll start to see and accept the heart that God has for healing.

Why are we often so surprised that God heals? Why is it weird to us when God does something supernatural? The answer is simple: either from experience, from what we've heard other people say about God, or just from our own reasoning, we as a Christian culture have formed a self-protecting view of God's power. Sure, we believe God has the power to heal, but for a myriad of reasons, we choose to believe that He's not going to heal us. In doing this, we're attempting to protect ourselves from disappointment.

I'm not trying to be insensitive. I understand that healing can raise feelings of anger and frustration. We all have that case in mind that allows us to ask the question, *If God still heals, then why hasn't He healed me—or why didn't He heal my friend or family member?* The reason sickness still occurs is because we still live in a sinful world. However, I'm not going to go into a deep theological explanation of why I believe God still heals. There are many resources out there that cover the topic. Instead, I'm going to talk about a few things God taught me about healing when I was in valley, and then I'm going to leave the rest up to you. If you have doubts about healing, please don't feel like I'm trying to condemn you. My heart is simply for you to receive whatever it is that God has for you. However, after reading this chapter, I encourage you to start a dialogue with God. Ask Him to reveal to you the truth behind this aspect of His character.

Earlier in this book, I talked about the healing I received while I was in the middle of the valley, and when I was praying for God to heal me of the pain and fatigue, I was thinking back to the day in college that I got so irritated that I chose to believe. By the time I entered the valley, my faith had been built up, almost in the way a child stacks blocks to build a stronger, taller tower. Even when we've experienced faith-building moments, doubts will almost always try to push their way back in.

After that moment in college, even though God had fixed my jaw-locking issue, a problem arose. I began to let myself think, *Well, I'll just wait a little longer before I admit that I have been healed.* How long is it going to take before you and I realize that God is a big God? I now choose to believe that God did heal my jaw that day, and no amount of time can prove it. My faith proves it. I'm not talking about a blatant denial of the facts, but instead I'm talking about a solid trust in the words that God has spoken to us. Listen to what Hebrews 11:1 says about faith:

"Now faith is the assurance of things hoped for, the conviction of things not seen."

I could go the rest of my life waiting to see if God has really healed my jaw, but I won't. I choose not to. I choose to thank God for healing me. *How can you be so sure?* I know who God is. I know Jesus, and because I know Him, I know what He has done, and I know what He is going to do. Many faith-preachers have treated healing as a magic formula—something that requires us to have enough faith or say the right phrase enough times—but it's not like that at all. Healing is not something we can manipulate God into doing. Healing is a gift that we, as children of God, can receive from our loving Father. It's based on a relationship, and it's available to us because of the grace of God—not because we have enough faith to receive it. Does it take faith to be healed? Yes. Jesus often told people in the New Testament that their faith had healed them, and He was correct. However, no amount of faith could possibly heal someone apart from the grace and power of God working on their behalf.

Jesus healed people because He had compassion on them, and He utilized the divine power of God to do it. The same way that our faith cannot save us apart from the grace of God, our faith cannot heal us apart from the grace of God. Our faith is simply a response to the promises that God has already made to His children in His word.

So, where does one get faith to actually receive healing? God has allotted us each a measure of faith, and one of the gifts of the Spirit is the gift of faith, but I also believe that faith can develop as your relationship with God grows. If you want more faith, read the Bible, but don't just read it to gain knowledge. Ask God to speak to you through His Word, and read it to grow your relationship with Him. I had the faith to believe that I could be healed just like the blind man crying out, "Have mercy on us," but I first had to read it. I first had to read the story before I could ever believe it, and as I read it, I allowed the Holy Spirit to make the words come alive to me—to speak to me through His Word. Romans 10:17 talks about this, and it says:

"So faith comes from hearing, and hearing by the word of Christ."

This verse isn't just talking about reading the Word. It's talking about a revelation of the Word that only happens when the Holy Spirit is speaking through what has been written. Many atheists have read the Bible and never gained any faith. We can't just read for knowledge. When we read the Word, it should be out of a response to the love of God, seeking to hear *from* Him and grow *in* Him.

I thought all we had to do was use the name of Jesus to be healed! There is power in the name of Jesus Christ, but the power in His name comes from His Spirit. If you don't have His Spirit, you can use His name all you want, and it won't do you any good. It's like a kid in school who always associates himself with the biggest and strongest kid in class. Anytime the other kids pick on him or mess with him, he simply says, "If you mess with me, Joe is gonna come get you." This may seem to work for a little while, but when Joe walks by while the kid is getting picked on, everyone is going to realize that the kid doesn't really know what he's talking about. He's going to say, "Don't mess with me or else Joe will beat you up," and Joe is going to say, "I don't know him."

However, if the kid takes the time to get to know Joe and to develop a friendship with him, then Joe is going to have his back. When he calls for Joe, Joe is going to say, "If you mess with him, you mess with me." So often, we try to throw around the name of Jesus to get out of stuff. We try to use His name to try and make things go our way. But do we really know the *person* behind the name, or do we just know the name?

When you truly know God, and have His Holy Spirit living inside of you, you are filled with power. You don't believe me? Jesus said in Acts 1:8:

"But you will receive power when the Holy Spirit has come upon you..."

Jesus isn't telling a joke—He's being serious. He isn't talking about the power to go to church or start attending a Bible study. He isn't talking about the power to sing songs or get in a spiritual mood. He's talking about the real, effective power of God. Paul says this in Romans 8:11:

"But if the Spirit of Him who raised Jesus from the dead dwells in you, He who raised Christ Jesus from the dead will also give life to your mortal bodies through His Spirit who dwells in you."

Wow. Paul isn't talking about the ordinary. He is saying that if the Holy Spirit lives in you, then you are filled with the same Spirit that raised Jesus from the dead. Jesus rising from the dead three days after He died (after having previously predicted His own resurrection) was God showing off His endless power.

That same power works in and through those who are filled with the Holy Spirit. Paul goes on to say that if this Spirit is in you, your body will be filled with life through His Spirit. God does not only desire to raise us up when Christ comes, He also wants to give life to our bodies now. Jesus didn't stop having compassion on sick people just because He ascended into heaven. He wants to give us life, and life to the full.

This raises a question about healing that I want to briefly address. If the power of God is available to us through the Holy Spirit, does that mean that God is going to heal every sickness every time? Yes and no. The best way to answer this is to compare healing with grace. God does want to save us from the presence of sin, and we experience that part of His rescue once we leave this earth and go to heaven. However, He also wants to save us from the power of sin now. By grace and through faith, we can have power over the strongholds of sin while on earth.

However, even if we access freedom from the power of sin, we still sometimes sin because we live in a sinful, fallen world. It's the same with healing. In heaven, there will be no sickness whatsoever. Also, by grace and through faith, it is possible for us to experience freedom from the power of sickness here on earth. However, even though we can experience freedom from the power of sickness, life is still not going to be perfect because we live in a fallen world.

I have not been healed every single time I asked, however, God has always addressed the issue when I have brought it before Him. He has never ignored me when I have cried out to Him. There have been many instances when I was healed immediately after praying. Other times, God has simply joined into conversation with me, showing me how He was planning on using my situation for His glory. For a little more Biblical backing on this subject, go read Psalm 103:3, which talks about God healing all our diseases. Also, look up what Paul says about the thorn in his flesh in 2 Corinthians 12:7-10. The best answer I can give you is this: sickness happens because of the effects of sin in the world, but God always addresses it in one way or another when we are walking in close relationship with Him. Even when we don't understand why something has been allowed to happen to us or to someone we love, God's goodness has not changed. He does not want us to needlessly suffer. He has a reason for everything He does *and* everything He allows. As we walk with Him, responding to His words in faith, He makes His power available to us through the Holy Spirit.

One time, a man was standing in a museum, intently studying an ancient sword that sat on display. As the man examined the sword, a mugger who often went around robbing people in public places walked up behind him. The mugger took a knife from his pocket and pointed it at the man studying the sword.

"Give me your wallet, now!" he barked with a muffled voice.

The man who had been studying the museum piece quickly grabbed the sword and pointed it back at the mugger. "Drop the knife," said the man.

The mugger looked confused and furious. "You can't do that," he said. "That's just a relic." The man holding the sword lifted it firmly and stuck it up to the mugger's neck, so that he could feel the blade press against his skin. "Drop the knife," he said again.

Especially in the American Christian church, we often put the power of God on display and out of use. We view it as nothing but a relic, and so we leave it to collect dust on a shelf. The truth is that we have been given power and authority through Jesus Christ. Matthew 28:18 says:

"And Jesus came up and spoke to them, saying, 'All authority has been given to Me in heaven and on earth.'"

From this statement, we know that Jesus had all the power of the Father abiding in Him. We can connect this truth to what Jesus says in John 14:14:

"If you ask Me anything in My name, I will do it."

We have already discussed what it means to use the name of Jesus. In order to speak the name with power, we have to know the *person* who owns the name. He has to be abiding in us. So, all the power and authority of God is living inside Jesus, and if we know

Him then Jesus is living inside us. How can we apply this to our health problems? Let me remind you that in Luke 10:19 Jesus says:

> *"Behold, I have given you authority to tread on serpents and scorpions, and over all the power of the enemy, and nothing will injure you."*

Let me put this together for you: Jesus has the power of God, Jesus will do anything we ask in His name, and Jesus has given us access to the same authority that was given to Him. I know some people argue that all these verses only applied to the disciples during Jesus' earthly ministry, and I know there are other reasons out there not to believe that they apply today. However, I'm also not trying to convince you with Scripture, because I know you could always find another Scripture with which to argue your point. I'm simply giving you the Scriptures that the Lord has given me when I needed healing, and I'm telling you that the reason I believe that God still heals is because I have experienced His healing.

So, if we have authority, then do we have the power to do whatever we want? Jesus gives us authority, not so that we can do what we want, but so that we can do whatever God wants. It's His power, not ours. To walk in authority, we need to learn to ask, *what does God want?* The easiest way to find out is to read His Word. Go read it for yourself. Go read the whole thing. God has filled His Word with powerful truths about His character and His plan, and if you will read and meditate on those truths, He will use His Word to help you walk in authority and power.

The best reason I can give for why God desires to heal you is because He loves you. I mentioned Romans 8:32 earlier in this book, but I want to show you what it says again.

> *"He who did not spare His own Son, but delivered Him over for us all, how will He not also with Him freely give us all things?"*

If you require healing, I have good news for you. God loves you so much that He sent His Son Jesus to suffer and die for you. Do you think that a God who loves you enough to save you from eternal damnation would not love you enough to heal your physical body? He loves you enough to free you from eternal suffering, so why is it so hard to believe that He wants to free you from your current suffering? Keep in mind, I'm not saying that healing happens when we pray just right or claim it just right. It starts with a relationship. It starts with belief.

In Mark 5, a woman who bled in her body for twelve years finally found healing when she, in faith, went to touch Jesus' garment. She believed the words that she heard about Jesus, and then she got close enough to Him to touch Him. Some of us wish Jesus would heal us, but we haven't believed the Word of God, and we haven't been willing to get close enough to Him to receive it. If you've been in that place, the best thing you can do is to begin to act on whatever faith you do have, even if it's the smallest amount. If you believe that God loves you, that's a great place to start. Seek Him with the belief that He loves you dearly, and pursue that relationship with Him, and I believe He will lead you to a place where you can hear directly from Him about His plan for your situation.

Do you remember me telling you about the night when I walked down my parents' road in pain? When I got out of bed that night, I did not have enough faith to be healed. I had enough faith to obey His leading, and I merely acted on the faith I had. I had enough faith to trust that, if I sought God, He would do something. I didn't know if I was going to be healed or not. All I knew was that He was going to do something when I pursued Him with all my heart. Use the faith God has given you. Start where you are, and God will take you to where you need to be.

When I was young, my dad and I were planning on tearing down an old metal swing set in our backyard. I grabbed some tools and began to head out back to take it apart, but my dad warned me not to start until he was out there to help me. I can't remember why I disobeyed and started taking it down by myself. Maybe I just wasn't thinking very clearly that day. Maybe I just didn't take him seriously. Either way, I didn't listen and I began to take it apart by myself.

I pulled myself up onto the metal ladder and reached up to loosen a bolt. As I yanked the wrench, my feet slipped and I fell straight down the ladder. Attempting to grab the metal pole as I fell, I caught my left thumb on a bolt that stuck out of the side of the ladder. The metal ripped right through my thumb. Bleeding all over my hands, I ran inside and went straight to the bathroom to wash it off. My thumb was cut clean open, but for some reason I tried to convince myself that it wasn't that bad. I thought, *Dad doesn't have to know about this.*

What's funny is we often try to hide our sins from God. What's worse is that we even try to hide the consequences from God, thinking that we are doing ourselves a favor. We don't want the added wrath of God on top of the consequences we have already received. But when my dad walked in the bathroom and saw my thumb, the last thing on his mind was, *I told you not to go out there and take it apart by yourself.* The first thing on his mind was, *My son needs help.*

I had been more worried about my father finding out what I had done than I was about the actual injury. Don't ever try to hide your injuries from God because you are afraid of Him finding out about your sin. God already knows. He already knows everything there is to know about you. Yes, we live in a fallen world, and we still deal with sickness and injury, but if you are a believer in Jesus, His blood has washed you clean of any guilt or shame regarding what you've done.

Your sickness is not punishment from God. He's not punishing you for your sins because Jesus already took the punishment on your behalf. If you're dealing with sickness, even if it's something that resulted because of a mistake you made, don't hide it from your Father. He loves you. You don't know how to fix yourself, but God knows how to fix you. He desires you to open up and give it all to Him.

We still need to be willing to receive the gentle discipline and conviction of the Lord, because God corrects those He loves. However, He's not going to use sickness, injury, or death to discipline us. How can I be sure? Sickness and death are results of sin, and God already put the payment for sin on the shoulders of Jesus. Matthew 8:17 makes this clear when it says:

"This was to fulfill what was spoken through Isaiah the prophet: 'He Himself took our infirmities and carried away our diseases.'"

When I look at my thumb now, it's easy to see that it functions just as well as my other fingers, but it will always bear a scar. That scar reminds me that my thumb is healed, but more importantly, that I am forgiven for the mistake I made. Thank God that the scars that your sin created are not on your body. They are on the hands and feet of Jesus.

GRACE

My relationship with God has been built on grace. Years after accepting Christ, I'm still daily amazed at the grace that God has shown me. I'm in awe at what He has done for undeserving people like myself. However, as much as God wants us to get grace, the devil wants us to miss it. Especially after we're saved, he tries to heap condemnation on us for sins that have already been covered. He's brought up my past so many times, telling me that I've made too many mistakes to receive the love of God, but God always breaks through the doubts with a reminder of His love and grace. As believers, we get to move forward in the grace of God because of the sacrifice of Jesus on the cross. As I walked through my own personal valley, God reinforced this truth in my life.

One night in particular, I was struggling with the fact that I was a sinner. Even though I had been saved, I still made mistakes from time to time, and the guilt and shame were pounding me from every side. So, I went before the Lord and said, *I feel like I'm not good enough, Jesus.*

I heard Jesus reply in my spirit. He gently said, *You're not. You don't need to be. I was good enough for you. And My grace is sufficient for you.*

The most important thing that I learned while struggling through the valley was this: God's grace is sufficient. There isn't anything we can do for ourselves. God has done everything for us through His Son Jesus. It is true that we are called to respond to the love of Jesus—to allow Him to continuously transform us—but we can find no justification without His sacrifice. When we accept real grace, God begins to change us into the image of His Son

Jesus Christ. But until you realize how much grace you have been given, you cannot truly begin to believe God about what He is going to do in your future. Until you accept the reality of the depth of the grace He has handed to you, you will not be able trust Him enough to allow Him to transform every part of you.

I'm not talking about hyper-grace, now. That's one of two things the devil tries to pervert grace into. He either tries to tell us that we have to earn our way into God's favor, or that God's grace just covers everything no matter if we ever come to a place of repentance and belief or not.

I believed the first lie for a long time as I grew up with a self-righteous works-based mindset. The latter of these two lies is what is known as hyper-grace. One version of it says that there is no need for repentance of sins, and this can lead to the idea that continuing in sin is okay, but this idea directly opposes the teachings of Christ. The devil wants us to swing too far one direction or too far the other, because his ultimate hope is that we'll miss the truth of amazing grace.

The truth is that God's grace is available to all people, but we have to accept it by coming to God in an attitude of repentance and believing in Jesus as our Lord and Savior. It's true that all you have to do is believe to get saved—there are verses like Acts 16:31 that state this directly—however, true belief in Jesus is always going to involve a repentant heart. God set it up so that repentance and belief would work hand-in-hand, and you cannot separate the two.

If you say, I'm a follower of Christ, but there's never repentance over sin, then I would question the legitimacy of your faith. Why? It has everything to do with the two natures that are at work. When we truly believe and are saved, we receive the nature of Christ. When His nature is working in us, we're not going to be okay with sin, because Jesus was not okay with sin. That brings me right back to what's so amazing about grace: Jesus was not okay with sin, but He loved sinners to the point of death. His goal was not to condemn the sinful. His goal was to save the lost, and that's the same thing He desires to do today.

Grace is amazing, but it's impossible to receive until we accept the fact that we need it. Before I was saved, I had a warped view of grace. I could clearly see that God was Holy, and I saw myself as nothing more than a gnat that had ticked Him off, and it scared me silly.

At that point, I had three options. I could try to make up for my sin (which is impossible), I could believe that sin had no consequences (which is a lie), or I could trust that God was loving, and that grace was a free gift that God had paid the highest price to offer us. It wasn't until I developed a healthy fear of God that I was able to recognize my need for grace, and it wasn't until I understood the love of God that I was able to accept it.

At the beginning of this book, I said that trusting God means becoming child-like. It's a funny way of putting it, but running to God really is a childish thing. Have you ever seen a young child do something wrong that caused their father to yell at them? I've seen it, and it's weird. It's weird to me because I'm an adult now. It doesn't make sense to me. The dad will be yelling at the kid, and the kid will run to the dad crying. Even while the dad is still yelling, the kid will wrap his or her arms around their father. Why do some children do this? What could possibly be running through their heads? I'll tell you what it is. That kid who runs to their dad trusts that their dad loves them. They know him, and they know that ultimately, he loves them despite their mistake. In the middle of their own mistake, they run to their father, believing that he will have compassion.

Maybe you didn't have the best father figure growing up. Maybe you didn't have one at all. You may have experienced anger or a lack of love in your house. You need to understand that God is not like that. He's not a father who hates us. He's not a father who leaves us and never comes back. He's not even a father who loves us yet still makes mistakes. He's a perfect Father, full of compassion and mercy. He's an endlessly loving Father, and He has grace that is sufficient for any failures you could ever bring to Him.

We need to be more like children. Jesus went so far as to say that we won't enter the kingdom of God until we become child-like. We need to begin to believe God with hearts that are completely surrendered to Him. We need to accept God's Word as truth, no matter how impossible His promises may seem. Jesus gave His life so that grace might be extended to us, but it's up to us to believe it.

When the lie of condemnation does surface, kick it back down where it belongs. Read through the gospels, jump up and down, and thank God for His sufficient grace. Do whatever you need to do to tell the lie that you're not buying into it. When we allow condemnation to sit around and fester, it convinces us that we need to start hiding things from God. Grace tells us that it's okay to lay our mistakes out before Him.

When you truly believe that His blood is enough, any sin you've been covering up gets swept away by a river of grace. Tell God about your sin—even if you feel like you've made the same mistake too many times. When you're willing lay it at His feet in repentance, His Spirit will remind you that it's already been forgiven. His Spirit will remind you that His grace is more than enough to cover it.

A young boy and his family moved into a new house. The boy was quite curious, so he went exploring deep into the woods behind their new backyard. One day, his mother told him about a certain swamp that sat half a mile away from their new home. She had heard from mothers in the neighborhood that it was a very dangerous place for children to go, so she gave her son strict orders not to go wandering into the swamp. Of course, being the curious boy that he was, he went down there to just take a look at the swamp.

It looked so inviting to a young boy of his age, so he decided to wade through it. During his adventure through the murky waters, he realized there were fish swimming all around him. He thought, "This is the perfect place to catch fish. I've got to come back here again."

Though, when he arrived home, he realized the muck on his clothes completely gave him away. His mother would see the mud and know right away that he had been playing in the swamp, so he took off his clothes and searched his room for a place to hide them. He discovered a panel in the wall that he could slide open and stuff his clothes into.

Every day after that, he would go playing in the swamp. Then he would go home and hide his clothes in the panel in the wall, thinking his mother would never find out. One day though, his conscience got the better of him. Also, he realized that he would eventually run out of clean clothes to wear.

Ashamed, he decided to tell his mother what he had been doing. He went downstairs and told her the whole story, and then he apologized for disobeying her.

"Thank you for being honest," she said.

"Will you still wash my dirty clothes?" he asked.

"You mean the ones covered in swamp water?" asked his mother. "I've already washed them. You kept throwing them down the laundry shoot, so I figured I would go ahead and take care of the mess simply because you are my son and I love you. Now don't go back to the swamp."

If you are born again, then your sins are paid for. If you truly are a child of God, the blood of Jesus has already washed you white as snow. When we allow our sins to pile up in our minds because we are afraid of what God will think, we are robbing ourselves of an extraordinary amount of grace. When Jesus said, "It is finished," it was finished right then and there. As soon as you believe in Him, you are set free and made new. Don't let yourself think that you can hide something from God. Bring it out into the open and let Him wash away the stain—not only from your soul, but also out of your life. His grace is like a detergent that cleanses perfectly. The love of God truly does cover a multitude of sins, and the grace of God really is sufficient.

- *15* -

Conclusion

If you want to truly find God, you have to spend time seeking Him. If you want to truly know Him, you have to spend *time* getting to know Him. I'm convinced that we as Christians make a decision not to seek God for one of two reasons. Either we don't really believe that we will find Him when we seek Him, or we don't really want to find Him because we know finding Him would mean allowing Him to change our lives. But it's not always going to be that way. We won't always be able to simply shove God to the back burner. One day, we are going to die, and God may ask us, *Why didn't you search for Me when I could be found?* God is a God of mercy. He's a God of love. He's a God of grace. Even now He is calling out to you, saying, *Seek Me and you will find Me, when you seek Me with all your heart.*

Ask yourself the question, *Do I really believe that the Creator of the universe loves me so much that He was willing to send His only begotten Son to die for me?* If the answer to this question is yes, then there ought to be a fire in your heart that compels you to do whatever it takes to be continuously walking by His side, to know Him, to understand what He wants from you, to seek after Him like there isn't anything holding you back, and to simply be in His presence no matter where that means you have to go.

The world relentlessly seeks after so many things. Those of us who know God should be relentlessly seeking after the One who gave everything for us. It's time for the Christian culture to change. It's time for believers to rise up and respond to the call of God. It's time for the redeemed children of God to seek after Him as if He was worth it—because He is. It's time for us to adapt an attitude of reverence for God—a healthy fear of the Lord. It's time for us to start believing that God loves us as much as He says He does. It's time for us to let go of these fleeting lives and choose to take up the life of Christ. It's time for us to trust that God is actually going to do what He says He is going to do.

I wish I had the passion to seek God, but the fire is just not there. How can I motivate myself to seek Him? That's a question worth asking, and I believe there's one answer that stands above the rest: encounter God's amazing love. Read about His love for you in the Bible, meditate on it, and memorize verses about it. Ask God specifically to reveal His love to you. When you truly experience His life-altering love, you can't help but seek after Him out of response to that love. His love motivated Jesus to die for me and you, and now, when we realize it for what it is, His love motivates us toward the calling of God on our lives as well. It motivates us to continue seeking Him. It compels us to continue walking the narrow road, treading after the footsteps of Christ.

Along with responding to the love of God, I would also measure the worth. Measure the worth of finding a true, living God who is going to forgive your every sin, provide for your every need, and give you a purpose that truly fulfills. If that's not worth it to you, then okay. But if it is worth it, seek Him simply because He *is* who He says He is. Seek Him simply because you believe He is going to do something. Seek Him simply because He is worthy.

When I seek God, I don't always feel like seeking Him. I don't always think, *Oh boy! I just can't wait to seek God with all my heart today!* Sometimes I feel that way, but other times I'm weighed down with the cares of the day. Here's what I've learned about seeking God: it's always a good idea, no matter how I feel in the moment. I often seek Him when I'm feeling my very worst. But I seek Him because I know what He is going to do. I seek Him because I have only ever found lasting peace and joy in His presence. I seek Him because I am nothing without Him. I seek Him because I know Him, and I want to be continuously closer to Him. I seek Him because He first came to seek and save me. That is what is so amazing about seeking God: the effort is not one-sided because God been passionately seeking us as well. Luke 19:10 says:

"For the Son of Man has come to seek and to save that which was lost."

I remember what it was like to be lost. I remember the hopelessness that comes with a life of sinful living. Jesus loved me too much to leave me in that place, so He came to seek me, and He didn't stop until He finished the job on the cross. In the end, we are unable to find God without going through Jesus Christ.

We could make countless sacrifices for God and never find Him if we choose to reject the gift of Jesus Christ. When you truly begin to believe that Jesus died for you and paid the highest price for your sins, your heart begins to burn with a fire for God. Perhaps you trusted God with your life a long time ago. If you can think back to what it was like to find Jesus, I challenge you to go back and remember. Remember the joy you felt. Remember the love you cherished—that an almighty God would really pay with His own Son's life to save you. I encourage you to remember, and to believe again.

If you're like I was though, you've never had that life-changing encounter with His love. Growing up, I thought I had always known Jesus as my Savior. Maybe you've just always considered yourself a Christian, and so you've never felt the need to seek after God. If this is you, then let me give you some good news. If you feel no desire to seek after God, then let me suggest that you may never have truly found God.

You call that good news? Yes, I call that good news. I call that good news because, if you are living a life empty of love for Christ, you are living an empty life. If you don't know Him on a personal level, and if He has never made a lasting change in your heart, then I humbly challenge your assumption that you have truly found Him.

Please don't get me wrong; I'm not trying to make you feel bad. I've simply been given a burden for people in the Christian church who have had a similar experience to me. Jesus said that some people would stand before Him and say, "Lord, Lord." Those are the "Christians" who never truly knew Him. My heart is not to condemn you. It's to encourage you. I don't want you to miss Jesus, because He's too good to miss. The good news is that you can receive Him right now by repenting of your sin and believing that Jesus paid the price for all of it. If you've gotten to this point in this book, and you still haven't done that, don't wait any longer. Nail it down now. I believe that God is reaching down to you right now, and He's saying, *Respond to My love. Respond to My grace. I'm opening the doors wide, and I'm inviting you into My family. Come in! Come in! It doesn't matter what you've done—my love can cover that when you turn away from it and turn to Me. Receive My Son, and come in.*

When you truly decide to seek God, you will find Him. When you seek God with all your heart, His Spirit fills you and you are never the same. Your heart wants to burst with excitement. Your eyes fill with tears because of the love that has been poured out upon you. Your passion is ignited and your purpose begins to be established. When you truly find God, your fear melts away and you find yourself resting in an ocean of peace and an atmosphere of joy.

When you find God, your confidence rises to once impossible heights—because you take on the confidence of Christ. When you find God, you begin to overflow with God—with His love and grace for others. When you truly find God, you want to run around and scream, "YEEEEEEEEEEEEEEEEEES!" at the top of your lungs. In that moment, you stop caring what other people think about you because there is Someone greater who thinks good thoughts about you. When you truly find God, you find real, lasting love—a perfect love. 1 John 4:18 attests to this. It says:

"There is no fear in love; but perfect love casts out fear, because fear involves punishment, and the one who fears is not perfected in love."

Fear involves punishment. The gospel summed up is simply that we deserved punishment, and Jesus took it all. We get to receive His grace by accepting what He's done for us—by accepting His words—by accepting Him. When we do that, His perfect love cast out all fear.

WHY GREAT THINGS ARE IN STORE

There have been moments when I'm sitting in God's presence, waiting on Him, when I'm given a glimpse—a picture—of His glory. It's as if God is giving me a foretaste of something we cannot fully see here on earth. I've seen an image in my spirit of that last day when the curtain will be pulled back and everything will come out into the light. When I consider judgment day, my first reaction is to think that God is going to list out my failures. I think I'm going to see everything sinful thing I ever did spread out before me.

Instead the picture I've seen during those moments in His presence is very different. I've found myself on a white shore. The waves of life are rushing behind me, but they're suddenly stilled. The sand is soft and warm. Beyond it is a small green hill of grass. After that is a thriving forest leading to a shining city. Everything in my view is filled with light. There isn't anything that isn't beautiful, and standing before me is Jesus Christ. He reaches out His hand and says, *You made it.* The love in His face is intense. It is perfect.

Now, I don't know what heaven is actually going to be like, because I have never been there. All I know for certain is what God has revealed to us in His Word. What I believe I have received from God is simply a visual representation of the peace and rest we will have in Him as we spend eternity in His presence. You see, my expectation of heaven has nearly always been filled with a dread of my sins coming into the light. For a long time, I feared what God would have to say when I finally stood before His throne. Now, I'm filled with a calming wonder at all that He has in store, and that peace comes from knowing that my sins are fully covered by the blood of Jesus. I can surely say that the grace of God has changed my life, and my eternity as well.

Now, if you've read this whole book up until now you may have a question like this running through your head: *What is the good plan you've been talking about this whole time? Throughout this whole book, you've been trying to convince me that God has this huge purpose for you to fulfill and that He was going to do great things in your life. What were those things? Have they happened?* I can only answer this question by simply saying this: when faith is in action, you can be just as sure at the beginning as you are at the end.

I have yet to see everything God is going to do in my life. I haven't experienced it all, but I believe that it will happen. I believe that God is telling the truth. And that's it.

That's the only evidence I have, unless—unless you were impacted by this book.

If God used the words on these pages to speak to you, then I believe it's because His plan for my life is already in motion. If while reading this, you have grown closer to God and have developed a greater desire to seek Him and more fully discover His great love, then God's purpose for my life is already in effect. If my words have inspired a growing passion in your heart for Jesus Christ, then God was telling the truth. I believe that He was, and more than that, I believe that He has a good plan for your life as well.

It's not like my life is completely free of doubt though. None of us can walk the Christian walk without doubting, but anytime doubt surfaces, I go straight back to His presence, and I allow the Holy Spirit to renew my strength. It was during one of these moments of renewal that the Holy Spirit encouraged me with these words: *I have great things in store for you. I don't have great things in store because you did the right things, said the right things, went the right places, met the right people, loved everyone enough, gave enough of your time, helped others enough, or laid down your life enough. I have great things in store for you because you know Me. I laid My life down for you so that you might have life. You have practiced My presence, and you have taken the time to come before Me. You have believed that what I said is true, and you have not stopped until you knew that Truth for yourself.*

There is a reason you can expect the good plan of God to follow a heart that is seeking after Him. The plan of God follows the presence of God, and you can come into His presence boldly because of the blood of Jesus. When you are first saved, His presence—the Holy Spirit—comes to live inside of you and gives life to your spirit. This is what Jesus meant when He said: "I will never leave you nor forsake you."

If you're asking, *Why don't I feel His presence?* or *Why have I been a Christian for such a long time and have never experienced the things you've been talking about?* The reason is simply because you haven't believed. As I've stated throughout this book, my goal is not to be harsh—I'm just trying to be honest. Jesus said in John 6:29:

"This is the work of God, that you believe in Him whom He has sent."

This not only means believing that God sent Jesus to die for us and that He was raised again. It also means believing the words He spoke. When we read the words, "I will never leave you nor forsake you," we can easily glance past the truth and think *well that's a nice sentiment.* The truth is this: if you're a believer, He will *never* leave you or forsake you. So, if you're saved and the Holy Spirit is in you, but you're not experiencing His work in your life, then what's the missing ingredient? When talking about the Holy Spirit, Jesus also said, "Ask and you shall receive." This is why belief is so important. If we don't believe the words of Christ, then we'll never get around to asking in faith. I encourage you to make a point to go read everything Jesus said. Don't just read it, though. Read it again and again, and ask God to speak to you. Read it, and then believe it.

Well, we're here at the end, but I want to leave you with one final picture. At one time, my life was like a chessboard sitting neatly organized on a shelf. One day, I bumped the shelf and the board and all the pieces came tumbling down. At first, I thought the game was ruined, but then as the pieces of my life fell, I stepped out in faith and began to trust in God. When you begin to trust in God with all your heart, He will begin to work out His good plan in your life. What once seemed like a sad ending will suddenly change into something new. For me, as I placed my hope in God, the chess board of life hit the table, and all the pieces began to land on the board in their proper positions and order.

This may sound impossible, but God says that nothing is impossible for those who believe. As you trust in God, you will watch to your amazement as everything lands in the position it was created to function in, and the best part is that your final location will be better than where you started. When you were once an old chessboard sitting unused on the shelf, now you have come to rest on the table, and the game has just gotten started.

Years later, after I finished the first draft of this book, I moved back home and married that girl from high school. That's a story for another time.

THANK YOU

Thank you for reading my testimony story. If you have enjoyed this book, please consider writing a review of *My Mess* on Amazon.com or GoodReads.com. I appreciate your review.

It takes considerable time and effort to create the books I publish and the videos I post. You can help support me by purchasing another copy of this book for a friend or loved one.

You can also show your support by purchasing a copy of my daily devotional, *30 Days of Inspiration and Hope*. Another way you can support my work is by donating monthly on Patreon.com/TroyBlack. I thank you for every bit of support that I receive and I pray that God has been able to bless you through this book.

In Christ,
Troy Black

Inspire Your Walk with Christ

How often do we look for hope in our circumstances instead of in Jesus? Walk with me for 30 days on a journey to know Jesus on a more personal level. Let His love and His Spirit renew your strength. I believe that with Jesus, there is always hope.

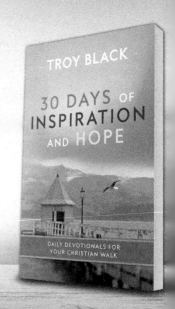

TROY BLACK

30 DAYS OF INSPIRATION AND HOPE

DAILY DEVOTIONALS FOR YOUR CHRISTIAN WALK

THE AUTHOR

Troy Black lives with his wife, Leslie, in East Texas. He likes board games, playing sports, reading, and going for long walks. Troy and Leslie have three daughters named Mirabelle, Iona, and Lauralee.

Troy and his wife started Inspire Christian Books out of a passion to spread the Gospel and the Truth of God's Word. It is their desire to see those who are lost come to salvation in Christ Jesus and for the Christian church to experience abundant life through the work of the Holy Spirit.

KEEP IN TOUCH

TroyBlackVideos.com
Facebook.com/AuthorTroyBlack
Youtube.com/InspireChristianBook

Made in the USA
Las Vegas, NV
16 May 2021

23171950R00105